THE BOOK OF

Graduation Wisdom

THE BOOK OF

Graduation Wisdom

INSPIRATIONAL ADVICE FOR LIFE FROM
MAYA ANGELOU, MARK TWAIN, COLIN POWELL,
ELEANOR ROOSEVELT, BILL GATES,
AND OVER 125 OTHER NOTABLES

Edited by Edward Hoffman, Ph.D.

CITADEL PRESS
Kensington Publishing Corp.
www.kensingtonbooks.com

CITADEL PRESS BOOKS are published by

Kensington Publishing Corp.
850 Third Avenue
New York, NY 10022

Copyright © 2003 Edward Hoffman

All Kensington titles, imprints, and distributed lines are available at special quantity discounts for bulk purchases for sales promotions, premiums, fund-raising, educational, or institutional use. Special book excerpts or customized printings can also be created to fit specific needs. For details, write or phone the office of the Kensington special sales manager: Kensington Publishing Corp., 850 Third Avenue, New York, NY 10022, attn: Special Sales Department, phone 1-800-221-2647.

CITADEL PRESS and the Citadel logo are Reg. U.S. Pat. & TM Off.

First printing: May 2003

10 9 8 7 6 5 4 3 2 1

Printed in the United States of America

Library of Congress Control Number: 2002115769

ISBN 0-8065-2485-5

To Eric, friend and colleague

CONTENTS

PREFACE

Graduation is typically a time of celebration and family joy. Together with marriage and childbirth, it now ranks among the most momentous events of our lives, and likewise marks a new beginning filled with promise and enthusiasm. Both high school and college graduation are also key times of transition, and linked therefore to issues involving decision-making, planning, and life-change.

Getting meaningful—especially inspirational—advice in our increasingly complex society is vital for today's graduates. Young men and women are faced with unprecedented choices for self-direction, career achievement, and community participation. In the new age of the Internet, opportunities are increasingly far-flung, even global. Due to massive changes in the organizational workplace, jobs and career ladders have become different as well. It would be no exaggeration to say that qualities of personal confidence, will, action, and vision have never been more crucial for both happiness and success. Yet little meaningful guidance has been directly offered to the millions of recent contemporary graduates—until now.

As a licensed psychologist for nearly twenty years and the father of two teenagers, I've witnessed both professionally and personally the import of graduation as a major life-event today. Having written biographies of prominent twentieth-century psychologists, and literary anthologies on such topics as fatherly advice and birthday sentiments, I felt the time was right to focus on "graduation wisdom"—that is, on guidance specifically intended for young men and women who have just reached this significant milestone.

Because the world of work and career has changed so much in the past decade, my emphasis in this anthology has been on current—rather than historically famous—leaders in various fields of achievement—ranging from science and technology to government and public affairs, literature, the arts, and entertainment. Nevertheless, in order to provide a historical backdrop to this lively collection of contemporary wisdom, I've included commencement selections from such celebrated American icons as Ralph Waldo Emerson, Theodore Roosevelt, Henry David Thoreau, and Mark Twain.

My wide-roaming literary research has proven both enjoyable and surprising. For example, I was fascinated to learn that it has been relatively recent—starting only about the year 1900—that colleges and universities have invited outside, "celebrity" figures in education, government, or business to address their graduates. Previously, the custom was to select a noteworthy student, faculty member, or administrator from within the institution to make a special speech. Indeed, it was in this context that Henry David Thoreau addressed his fellow Harvard graduates in 1837 in a stirring selection excerpted in this book. Likewise, I was intrigued to discover that such English-speaking nations as Britain and Canada have never followed our tradition of the inspirational graduation speech—a facet of higher education that is now so ingrained as to be parodied in countless American magazines, movies, and TV shows.

Keeping in mind the issue of relevance, I've sought to feature advice that virtually every new graduate will find helpful and beneficial. No matter whether he or she intends a career in business or the arts, education or public service, technology or health care, these wise remarks about such matters as self-knowledge and integrity, cultivating experience and perseverance, appreciating parents, contributing to the world, dreaming, learning, playing, and goal-setting are superbly germane to every new graduate's life. And come to think of it, to all their family members, too—whatever their chronological age or particular accomplishments.

Similar in format to *The Book of Fathers' Wisdom* and *The Book of Birthday Wishes,* I've provided a biographical sketch of each contributor. Reflecting the contemporary focus of this book, most of the figures are well known and therefore require minimal introduction. Except where otherwise clearly stated in the text, all one hundred thirty seven selections are excerpted from college, and occasionally high school, commencement ceremonies. In the end section of this anthology, I've detailed the specific place and year.

The Book of Graduation Wisdom has been a true "garden of delight" to research and edit. It's my hope that these rays of insight will illumine the lives of new graduates everywhere with clarity, vision, and purpose.

ACKNOWLEDGMENTS

This book would scarcely have been possible without the valuable help of many people. The enthusiasm of my agent, Alice Fried Martell, was instrumental in bringing this project to the attention of editor Bob Shuman, whose literary judgment and organizational skill are much appreciated. Assistant editor Miles Lott ably guided the manuscript through to production. For their encouragement and conceptual contributions on this anthology's theme, I'm much indebted to Fannie Cheng, Eric Freedman, Dr. Ted Mann, Elaine Akemi Oshiro, and Paul Palnik. In providing research assistance, Harvey Gitlin, Linda Joyce, and Mia Song again have proven efficient. From start to finish, my family was also a source of lively encouragement and unflagging support.

ACKNOWLEDGMENTS

THE BOOK OF

Graduation
Wisdom

Accepting Life's Vicissitudes

Billy Joel

An icon of pop music since the mid-1970s, Billy Joel was raised on New York's Long Island and dropped out of high school just short of graduation to follow his love of music. His early projects proved less than successful, but he made it into the ranks of chart-toppers by writing and performing songs that included "Movin' Out (Anthony's Song)," "Just the Way You Are," "She's Always a Woman," and "Only the Good Die Young." Although his massive fortune and high-profile failed marriage to model Christie Brinkley might suggest otherwise, Joel has kept his status as a working-class hero throughout his career, infusing his songs with tales of family life and giving tribute to the local institutions that saw his rise to fame.

I became a performing artist, a recording artist, a rock and roll star, through pure serendipity. I originally wanted to be a songwriter, a composer. I don't know of any special formula that will ensure great personal fortune. Hell, I lost as much money as I made over the years. I think that good luck and good timing are probably just as important as a good education, although owning some nice waterfront property out here didn't hurt.

I never studied the law and I never took any accounting courses, although I sure as hell could have used the knowledge of both in my life. I didn't graduate from high school, but here I am being given my fourth doctorate. It's honorary, of course. But it still looks nice on the wall, and that and an E-Z pass will get me over the Triboro Bridge.

I congratulate you all for staying with your academic pursuits. I couldn't do it. And now I wish I had studied more myself. It would help me in my own musical efforts these days. . . . I am certain of only one thing in my life. I knew what I loved to do, and I did what I love to do. I never did it to make a lot of money. I did it to make a living. And in doing so, I made a life. My job became my friend, my fortune, and my great love.

No matter what lofty goals I set for myself, life came along and whacked me upside the head and sent me in directions I never intended to go. But I learned to adjust. I used the survival lessons as substance for future material.

Andrew Rooney

"The most felicitous nonfiction writer in television" is how *Time* once described Andrew Rooney, the CBS News correspondent, writer, and producer. Six-time winner of the Writers Guild Award for Best Script of the Year, Rooney grew up in Albany, New York, and flew with the Eighth Air Force on the first American bombing raid over Germany. His twelve books include *Air Gunner: The Story of the Stars and Stripes, Conquerer's Peace,* and *Fortunes of War.*

One of the things you have to face . . . is the unpleasant fact that you will not ever arrive at any condition of life with which you are totally satisfied and happy. It seems unfortunate, but it's true, that to experience real happiness, you first, or occasionally anyway, have to be unhappy. So you're going to be unhappy, sometimes. Just accept it as part of the process. Ambition and satisfaction are at war. If you're ambitious, you aren't satisfied, and if you're satisfied, you aren't ambitious.

Most of us are plagued by ambition. It's one of the best and worst things about us. . . . I've been successful and it's satisfying, but the best parts of my life are the small, day-to-day pleasures—a drink of cold water, the newspaper in the driveway, beating someone away from a traffic light. I take more enjoyment from sitting at my desk writing then I take from the money it brings in. That's a good thing because I write every day, but I get paid only once every two weeks.

Achieving Academic Success

JACK LONDON

Born in late-nineteenth-century San Francisco, Jack London was one of America's most popular authors. His novels included *The Call of the Wild, White Fang,* and *The Sea Wolf.* He had strong but contradictory attitudes about individual achievement and societal improvement. After his stormy marriage ended, London kept up a relationship—often strained—with his daughter Joan mainly through correspondence.

Writing from his ranch at Glen Ellen, California, in May 1913, London sent his daughter this academic advice:

Dearest Joan:

English, French and Algebra are all right.
First year, by all means take Ancient History.
Second year, by all means take Medieval and Modern History.
By all means, don't overwork.
Be sure to plan for one year of science when it comes along.

Love—Congratulations—Daddy

Achieving Racial Justice

Lyndon Johnson

The thirty-sixth president of the United States grew up in small-town Texas. His father was initially a successful and much-admired state politician, but the family sank into near-poverty in the mid-1920s due to poor business conditions. Though Johnson's presidency was indelibly marred by his huge expansion of U.S. involvement in the Vietnam War, his legacy on civil rights—including vigorous lobbying of Congress to win passage of the landmark 1964 Civil Rights Act—is probably his greatest achievement.

What is justice? It is to fulfill the fair expectations of man. Thus, American justice is a very special thing. For, from the first, this has been a land of towering expectations. It was to be a nation where each man could be ruled by the common consent of all—enshrined in law, given life by institutions, guided by men themselves subject to its rule. And all—all of every station and origin—would be touched equally in obligation and in liberty.

Beyond the law, lay the land. It was a rich land, glowing with more abundant promise than man had ever seen. Here, unlike any place yet known, all were to share the harvest.

And beyond this was the dignity of man. Each could become whatever his qualities of mind and spirit would permit—to strive, to seek, and, if he could, to find his happiness. This is American justice. We have pursued it faithfully to the edge of our imperfections, and we have failed to find it for the American Negro.

So, it is the glorious opportunity of this generation to end the one huge wrong of the American Nation, and in so doing, to find America for ourselves, with the same immense thrill of discovery which gripped those who first began to realize that here, at last, was a home for freedom.

Admiring Small Communities

ANDREW YOUNG

Andrew Young's career as a civil rights activist and public official has spanned more than forty years. Raised in New Orleans, he became a minister and in 1960 joined the Southern Christian Leadership Conference spearheaded by Dr. Martin Luther King, Jr. The two worked together closely, and as the group's executive director (1964–1970) Young took an active role in ending segregation throughout the South. Shortly thereafter, he became the first African American to represent Georgia in Congress since 1871 and served under President Jimmy Carter as U.S. representative to the United Nations. Holding office as mayor of Atlanta for eight years, Young remains a national figure within the African American community.

I think the happiest times I have spent in my childhood have been in small towns. The love and family atmosphere at this small college probably contributed more to your education than you realize. You will come to appreciate the size of this campus and the fact that people know your name and that people care about you. This is an extended family that will go on with you forever. Many college graduates this spring will receive the same degree as you do today, yet they will not receive it with the love and prayer and commitment you are taking from this college.

These are qualities that come from being just the right size. Transforming the megalopolis to right-sized communities is going to be done by people who are committed to translating the ideals of their lives into the lives of their neighbors.

Advancing the Democratic Experiment

RONALD REAGAN

The fortieth president of the United States was frequently derided in the press for his seemingly simplistic approach to domestic issues and especially a strongly anti-Soviet foreign policy. In ensuing years, however, historians have increasingly come to see Reagan as an original thinker with a carefully honed vision of American democracy and its unfulfilled potential in a world still dominated by authoritarian governments and ideologies.

This nation was born when a band of men, the Founding Fathers, as a group so unique we've never seen their like since, rose to such selfless heights. Lawyers, tradesmen, merchants, farmers—fifty-six men achieved security and standing in life but valued freedom more. They pledged their lives, their fortunes, and their sacred honor. Sixteen of them gave their lives. Most gave their fortunes. All preserved their sacred honor. They gave us more than a nation. They brought to all mankind for the first time the concept that man was born free, that each of us has inalienable rights, ours by the grace of God, and that government was created by us for our convenience, having only the powers that we choose to give it.

This is the heritage that you're about to claim as you come out to join the society made up of those who have preceded you by a few years, or some of us by a great many.

This experiment in man's relation to man is a few years into its third century. Saying that might make it sound quite old. But let's look at it from another viewpoint or perspective. A few years ago, someone figured out that if you could condense the entire history of life on earth into a motion picture that would run for twenty-four hours a day, three hundred sixty-five days [a year]—maybe on leap years we could have an intermission—this idea is that the United States wouldn't appear on the screen until three-and-a-half seconds before midnight on December 31. And in those three-and-a-half seconds, not only would a concept of society come into being—a golden hope for all mankind—but more than half the activity, economic activity in world history, would take place on this continent.

Free to express their genius, individual Americans, men and women, in three-and-a-half seconds, would perform such miracles of invention, construction, and production as the world had never seen.

Affirming Childlike Qualities

STEVEN SPIELBERG

Steven Spielberg is undoubtedly the most popular filmmaker in the world today. He grew up in a middle-class Jewish family in Cincinnati during the 1950s, and received encouragement from his doting mother to pursue imaginative and creative activities. Since the age of twenty-eight, with his blockbuster *Jaws,* Spielberg has directed a series of hugely profitable and aesthetically acclaimed movies including *Close Encounters of the Third Kind, E.T., Raiders of the Lost Ark, The Color Purple, Jurassic Park, Schindler's List,* and *Minority Report.*

My films have been often accused of—or, as I like to think, applauded for, having childlike qualities. I do believe that the greatest quality that we can possess is curiosity, a genuine interest in the world around us. The most used word—and I have five kids, so I know what I'm talking about—the most used word in a child's vocabulary is "Why?" From this simple question and such basic curiosity, great acts are born. . . .

The child's brave spirit is the angel inside each of us, the force that often seems to shrink as we grow bigger. Still, it's there, and we have a responsibility to keep it strong, just as we work our bodies to keep the muscles from atrophying. It doesn't matter what path we take; we have to remain curious and fearless.

Allowing Yourself to Be Celebrated

WHOOPI GOLDBERG

One of Hollywood's and Broadway's leading actresses today is Whoopi Goldberg. Born Caryn Johnson in New York City, she spent her early years living in a drug-laden housing project before making her performing debut at age eight with the Helena Rubenstein Children's Theatre at the Hudson Guild. After dropping out of high school, she found work as a summer camp counselor, and in the choruses of 1970s Broadway shows like *Hair, Pippin,* and *Jesus Christ, Superstar.*

Whoopi's film career ignited when director Steven Spielberg cast her in the leading role in *The Color Purple,* based on Alice Walker's novel. She won an Academy Award for her acting in the hugely successful movie *Ghost,* and ever since has been a prolific presence on stage, TV, and screen. Whoopi is also well known for her activism on behalf of many charitable and social organizations, and her openness about her impoverished origins.

The world now is about pause—before you speak, before you pass judgment, before you decide what somebody else is not, check your own basket. If you hear nothing else today, if you take nothing else with you, before you go to make that judgment, check your own basket. Because what you say and how you act toward people [have] taken on new meaning.

We are going to get older, but what counts as we age is: are we better? Facial stuff. It falls. That's why they have Botox commercials, honey. Physical? It can go away like that! [Your] chest will fall. Backside will get bigger. Those things, they're kind of nice for two years. I admit it. But who you are beyond all of that is the most difficult task you have. *Being yourself is going to be the hardest thing you do in life.*

Allow yourselves to be celebrated. Allow [your family] to take great pleasure in your accomplishment because they're living a little through you. And by God, look at what you've given them. Look at what you did! Everybody always says, "Oh, the youth of today, they can't do anything." You did it! You did it! Just for a second, turn around and look at each other. You did it!

Appreciating Language

J.R.R. TOLKIEN

Not for fame or wealth did J.R.R. Tolkien write fantasy epics like *The Hobbit* and *The Lord of the Rings* trilogy. Rather, Tolkien wanted to entertain the four children that he and his wife, Mabel, were raising in Oxford, where he taught medieval languages. As orphans, both wanted the kind of close, loving family life they had never personally known.

Tolkien was able to give his children the gifts of his prodigious imagination by inventing fantasy tales for their amusement. While writing *The Hobbit,* Tolkien avidly solicited their advice about its developing plot and characters. Even after garnering international renown, he maintained a modest, quiet lifestyle at Oxford, and kept scholarly allegiance to his field of language study.

I have once or twice, not so long ago, been asked to explain or defend this *language*: to say how it can possibly be profitable or enjoyable. As if I were some curious wizard with arcane knowledge, with a secret recipe that I was unwilling to divulge.

To compare the less with the greater, is not that rather like asking an astronomer what he finds in mathematics? Or a theologian what is the interest of the textual criticism of Scripture? As in Andrew Lang's fable a missionary turned on a critic with the words: "Did Paul know Greek?"

I did not accept the challenge. I did not answer, for I knew no answer that would not appear uncivil. But I must have said: "If you do not know any language, learn some—or try to. You should have done so long ago. The knowledge is not hidden. If you cannot learn, or find the stuff distasteful, then keep humbly quiet. You are a deaf man at a concert. If you do not specially enjoy old wine of a good vintage, drink some. Drink again. Persevere. Take it with your other meats—and perhaps cut down on whiskey!"

Grammar is for all, though not all may rise to star-spangled grammar.

Appreciating Parental Pride

GARRISON KEILLOR

Garrison Keillor is best known as the originator and host of *A Prairie Home Companion,* the radio show centered on the events of the fictitious Minnesota town of Lake Wobegon. The program, which ran on more than two hundred stations on the American Public Radio network, received a Peabody Award in 1981 and a Grammy in 1987. As a radio host, he continues to bring folksy wit and humor to the airwaves.

Parents are cheerful and forward-looking people. We are inherently hopeful. And we looked forward to the time when you walked, and to your first words, and to your first sentences. Some of you, we're still looking forward to your first good paragraph, but we're hopeful.

We are inherently looking out for the best. We are terribly proud of you, and we always were, although we've tried to be tasteful about it. And not to constantly talk about you while you're present. If this were not commencement at Gettysburg College, but instead were visiting day at the state prison, and we were here to bring you fruit and some magazines, we would still be proud of you—though we're grateful for the difference. A life behind bars is something that's been contemplated by every parent.

Asking the Big Questions

JODIE FOSTER

Starring in such popular films as *Contact* and *The Silence of the Lambs,* Jodie Foster is among the world's leading actresses today. Raised in Los Angeles by a financially hard-pressed mother, "Little Jodie," as she was called often depended on her siblings for nurturing. Her career was launched when, at the age of three, she successfully auditioned for Coppertone. By the age of fifteen, under her mother's skillful management, Jodie had appeared in more than fifty television shows including *Bonanza, Gunsmoke,* and *The Partridge Family* and starred as a child actress in the movies *Alice Doesn't Live Here Anymore* and *Taxi Driver,* for which she won an Oscar nomination in 1976. After studying acting at Yale, Jodie appeared in a variety of well-received films including *The Panic Room, Sommersby, Nell,* and *Home for the Holidays* and *Little Man Tate,* both of which she directed.

The big questions: What is pleasure, what is pain, what is trust, what is authentic, what is merely convention? What is a completely ridiculous lie? Who are my parents? Where do they stop and where do I begin? Who are my lovers? Where do they stop and where do I begin? Who are my mentors, my family, and my enemies? Where do I stop and where do they begin? What is certainty? What is deception, how do I feel, in here, in here and out there? . . .

How does the "I" get better instead of worse? How does it reveal its character more fully as opposed to settling for an approximate shape? How does the "I" leave its mark on the world as proof of having existed? In my case, those questions came immediately after graduation, after I spent my requisite six months of depression, lying in bed for fourteen hours a day, not wanting to ask the next big question. . . . And somewhere between a lot of naps and some late-night reruns, I found something to get very passionate about: my work. I often say that in my life there are only three things: love, work, and family. And I've been lucky to occasionally find all three in my job. . . .

Avoid Conformity

MARTIN LUTHER KING, JR.

Martin Luther King, Jr. was the most important civil rights leader of our time. Raised in Montgomery, Alabama, and ordained as a minister in 1957, King was a charismatic speaker, tireless organizer, and inspiring activist. His momentous "I have a dream" speech delivered before hundreds of thousands of supporters at the 1963 March on Washington was a turning point in our nation's history. At the time of his assassination at age thirty-nine in 1968, King was already seeking to build a broader national and international agenda for justice and world peace.

Every academic discipline has its technical nomenclature, and modern psychology has a word that is used, probably more than any other. It is the word *maladjusted*. This word is the raging cry of modern child psychology. Certainly all of us want to live a well-adjusted life in order to avoid the neurotic personality. But I say to you, there are certain things within our social order to which I am proud to be maladjusted and to which I call upon all men of goodwill to be maladjusted.

If you will allow the preacher in me to come out now, let me say to you that I never did intend to adjust to the evils of segregation and discrimination. I never did intend to adjust myself to religious bigotry.

I never did intend to adjust myself to economic conditions that will take necessities from the many to give luxuries to the few. I never did intend to adjust myself to the madness of militarism, and the self-defeating effects of physical violence. And I call upon all men of goodwill to be maladjusted because it may well be that the salvation of our world lies in the hands of the maladjusted.

Avoid Negative Thoughts

HENRY WINKLER

With a comic acting career spanning a quarter century, Henry Winkler is undoubtedly best known for playing "the Fonz"—character Arthur Fonzarelli—on the 1970s hit TV series *Happy Days*. Raised in New York City, Winkler studied drama at Emerson College and later at Yale. His recent movies have included *The One and Only, Down to You, Little Nicky,* and *The Waterboy*.

Allowing negative thoughts to live in your mind and body is powerful and addictive. What I have learned is that there is no nutritional value in a negative thought. Those negative thoughts that live in your mind and in your soul, they pervade every part of your life. And you know those thoughts: "I'll never," "She won't go out with me," "He won't go out with me," "I'll never get that job," "I'll never achieve," "I'll never," "I won't be able to," "I can't," "It will never happen."

When those thoughts come into your mind, you say [to them], "I'm sorry, I have no time for you now." If you put a period at the end of a negative thought, it will become a paragraph, and that paragraph will become a thesis of negativity that will hold you in your place.

And if you say, "I have no time for you now," and if you make that a part of your ritual—if you don't put a period at the end of that negative thought, it will leave you. And you will continue your march toward your dream. I am living proof. "If you will it, it is not a dream."

Avoid Obsessing About Money

STEPHEN KING

Stephen King is among the world's most popular writers, and undoubtedly the leading horror writer of our time. His more than forty books include a four-part series of novels, a six-part serial novel, and numerous short stories. These include *Everything's Eventual, Dreamcatcher, Hearts in Atlantis,* and *From a Buick 8.* Despite his fame and wealth, King has spent most of his professional life quietly residing in his native Maine. King made international news in 1999 when he was nearly killed in a hit-and-run accident near his rural home.

What will you do? Well, I'll tell you one thing you're not going to do, and that's take it with you. I'm worth I don't know exactly how many millions of dollars—I'm still in the Third World compared to Bill Gates—but on the whole I'm doing okay, and a couple of years ago I found out what "you can't take it with you" means. I found out while I was lying in the ditch at the side of a country road, covered with mud and blood and with the tibia of my right leg poking out the side of my jeans like the branch of a tree taken down in a thunderstorm. I had a MasterCard in my pocket, but when you're lying in the ditch with broken glass in your hair, no one accepts MasterCard. . . .

We all know that life is ephemeral, but on that particular day and in the months that followed, I got a painful but extremely valuable look at life's simple backstage truths. We come in naked and broke. We may be dressed when we go out, but we're just as broke. Warren Buffet? Going to go out broke. Bill Gates? Going to go out broke. Tom Hanks? Going out broke. President Fergusson? Broke. Steve King? Broke. You guys? Broke. Not a crying dime. And how long in between? How long have you got to be in the chips? . . . Just the blink of an eye. . . .

Should you give away what you have? Of course, you should. I want you to consider making your lives one long gift to others, and why not? All you have is on loan, anyway.

Be Adventurous

SALMAN RUSHDIE

Raised in Bombay in a middle-class Muslim family, novelist Salman Rushdie became an international cause célèbre upon being condemned to death by the former Iranian spiritual leader Ayatollah Ruholla Khomeini in 1989. The Nobel Prize–winning writer had incurred this wrath for his novel *The Satanic Verses,* which contained material deemed heretical. After the religious decree *(fatwa),* Rushdie went into hiding but continued to produce books, including *In Good Faith, Imaginary Homelands, The Moor's Last Sigh,* and *Mirrowork.* Although some Muslim clerics have continued to offer bounties for Rushdie's death, in 1998 the Iranian government announced that it would not put the *fatwa* into effect or encourage anyone to do so. As a result, Rushdie has taken greater liberties in public appearances, such as this commencement:

It is men and women who have made the world, and they have made it in spite of their gods. The message of the myths is not the one the gods would have us learn—that we should behave ourselves and know our place—but its exact opposite. It is that we must be guided by our natures. Our worst natures can, it's true, be arrogant, venal, corrupt, or selfish; but in our best selves, we—that is, you—can and will be joyous, adventurous, cheeky, creative, inquisitive, demanding, competitive, loving, and defiant.

Do not bow your heads. Do not know your place. Defy the gods. You will be astonished how many of them turn out to have feet of clay. Be guided, if possible, by your better natures. Great good luck and many congratulations to you all.

Become a Dreamer

Toni Morrison

Toni Morrison is the first African American woman to be awarded the Nobel Prize for Literature, in 1993. Her twelve books include *Tar Baby, Song of Solomon, Jazz, The Dancing Mind,* and *The Big Box.* Since 1988, Morrison has been a professor at Princeton University and chaired its Creative Writing Program. When asked by a student "who she wrote for," Morrison swiftly replied: "I want to write for people like me, which is to say black people, curious people, demanding people—people who can't be faked, who don't need to be patronized, and who have very, very high criteria."

I want to talk about dreaming. Not the activity of the sleeping brain, but rather the activity of an awake and alert one. Not idle, wishful speculation but engaged, directed daytime vision. Entrance into another space—someone else's situation, sphere, projection, if you like. By dreaming, the self permits intimacy with the other without the risk of being the other. And this intimacy that comes from pointed imagining, should precede all of our decision-making, all of our cause-mongering and our action.

Becoming a Conscious Parent

ANNA QUINDLEN

Since the age of twenty-five, Anna Quindlen has been among the most influential American journalists. In 1992, she won a Pulitzer Prize for her columns as a *New York Times* writer, a post she left several years later to pursue a novelistic career. Her works of fiction include *Siblings, Naked Babies, Happily Ever After,* and *Against the Heart,* which was adapted into a film starring Meryl Streep and William Hurt. Today, Quindlen continues in her journalistic role as a regular columnist for *Newsweek.*

We parents have forgotten our way sometimes. When you were first born—each of you—our great glory was in thinking you absolutely distinct from every baby who had ever been born before. You were a miracle of singularity, and we knew it in every fiber of our being. You shouted, "Dog." You lurched across the playground. You put a scrawl of red paint next to a squiggle of green and we put it on the fridge and said, "Oh, my God, oh, my God, you are a painter, a poet, a prodigy, a genius."

But we are only human, and being a parent is a very difficult job, more difficult than any other, because it is 24/7, because it is unpaid and unrewarded much of the time, because it requires the shaping of other people, which is an act of extraordinary hubris.

And over the years, we learned to want for you things that you did not necessarily want for yourself. We learned to want the lead in the play, the acceptance to our own college, the straight and narrow path that sometimes leads absolutely nowhere. We learned to suspect, even fear your differences, not to celebrate them. Sometimes we were convinced conformity would make life better, or at least easier, for you. Sometimes we had a hard time figuring out where you ended and we began.

Guide us back to where we started. Help us not to make mistakes out of fear or out of love. Teach us gently as we once taught you, about who you really are and what you intend to become. Learn not to listen to us when we are wrong. Whether you are twenty-four or fifty-four, begin today to say "No" to the Greek chorus that thinks it knows the parameters of a happy life when all it knows is the homogenization of human experience. . . .

You are only real if you can see yourself clear and true in the mirror of your soul and smile upon the reflection.

AL FRANKEN

As a founder of *Saturday Night Live* in the 1970s, Franken won five Emmys, four for writing and one for producing. After a respite, he returned to the program in 1985 for another decade, in which he developed his most popular character, self-help guru Stuart Smalley. His recent film projects have included *When a Man Loves a Woman*, *Stuart Saves His Family*, and the HBO miniseries *From the Earth to the Moon*. Also a well-known political satirist, Franken has authored several books, including *Why Not Me?* and *Oh, the Things I Know: A Guide to Success, or Failing That, Happiness.*

Parenting is the hardest job you'll ever love. First and foremost, being a good parent means spending lots of time with your children. I personally hate the phrase "Quality Time." Kids don't want Quality Time, they want Quantity Time—big, stinking, lazy, nonproductive Quantity Time. On the other hand, it's important for every parent to maintain balance in his or her life. Don't be a slave to your child. No one respects a slave—unless he's played by Morgan Freeman.

Becoming a Good Conversationalist

WILLIAM GASS

William Gass is the author of complex novels including *The Tunnel* and *Omensetter's Luck,* and works of literary criticism such as *Habitations of the World* and *Tests of Time.* A professor of philosophy at Washington University since 1969, Gass is known for his witty yet passionate defense of literature's freedom of expression. "The only holy word," he has written, "is the free word."

On this beautiful ceremonial morning, I want to talk to you about talking, that commonest of all our intended activities, for talking is our public link with one another; it is a need, it is an art, it is the chief instrument of all instruction; it is the most personal aspect of our private life.

To those who have sponsored our appearance in the world, the first memorable moment to follow our inaugural bawl is the birth of our first word. It is that noise, a sound that is no longer a simple signal, like the greedy squalling of a gull, but a declaration of the incipient presence of mind, that delivers us into the human realm. Before, there was only an organ of energy, intake, and excretion, but now a person has begun. And in no idle, ordinary or jesting sense, words are what being will become. It is language which most shows a man.

Becoming a Hero

BARRY LEVINSON

Barry Levinson is among Hollywood's leading writers and directors. His best-known films include *Rain Man, Young Sherlock Holmes, Good Morning, Vietnam* and *Sleepers*. Set in his native Baltimore, Levinson's two "personal" movies in theme—*Diner* and *Avalon*—both won Oscar nominations for Best Screenplay.

We may not have a world of heroes anymore because television demystifies everyone. No one is as good as we had hoped, but what does that mean for you, this class today, when you can't look to others for the answers or the heroes?

The heroes in the future are going to have to be you. You are going to have to demand more from this society than you live in, you are going to have to demand more from the politicians, more from all the institutions to do better work. Ultimately, you are going to have to take that responsibility as parents raising children, making a community that is more responsible, schools that are more responsible to individuals that may need that. But here is where the heroes can begin.

You will have a professional life and a private life, and you are going to have to mix the two [to] benefit you, your family, your community, your country, and it starts here. For me, the future begins here.

Becoming a Lawyer

ART BUCHWALD

Art Buchwald is a Pulitzer Prize–winning journalist based in Washington, D.C. He peddled magazines on New York street corners during the Depression and lived in foster homes. After serving in World War II, he enrolled in college and eventually traveled to Paris, where he lived for fourteen years. Syndicated since 1952, his popular column of political satire has appeared in more than five hundred thirty newspapers.

I am no stranger to the law. I first became interested in the law when I was working in Paris for the *Herald Tribune,* and I covered a trial which had to do with a couple caught in a very compromising situation in a Volkswagen. Now, everyone in France was interested in the case because it had to do with such a small car. The defense lawyer argued it was impossible to do what the couple had been accused of doing in a Volkswagen. The judge said he didn't know if this was true or not, so he appointed a commission to study it. It took them six months to render their verdict, and they said: "It was possible but very difficult."

What does a speaker say to a fresh-faced, well-scrubbed graduating class of neophyte lawyers? Your studies are over, and now you will leave these hallowed halls, this ivy-covered campus, to go out and practice the second oldest profession in the world.

Becoming a Musician

DAVID BOWIE

Estimated to be the wealthiest rock star in Britain today, Bowie was born David Robert Jones in 1947 London. The son of a working-class family, he began rhythm-and-blues on the saxophone at the age of twelve, but didn't seriously consider a musical career until after graduating from technical school with an art degree. Adopting the stage name David Bowie, he gained international fame in the 1970s with such albums as *Ziggy Stardust, Diamond Dogs,* and *Young Americans.* During the same period, Bowie starred in the science-fiction film *The Man Who Fell to Earth.* Ever since, he has continued to produce and perform with various bands, and in 1996 was inducted into the Rock and Roll Hall of Fame.

As always on occasions like this, I really never know what to do—which is pretty much the way that I've handled my career as a musician/writer. I guess any list of advice I have to offer a musician always ends with, "If it itches, go and see a doctor." Real world! But that's not going to be of any help today. . . .

Music has given me over forty years of extraordinary experiences. I can't say that life's pains or more tragic episodes have been diminished because of it. But it's allowed me so many moments of companionship when I've been lonely and a sublime means of communication when I wanted to touch people. It has been both my doorway of perception and the house I live in. I only hope that music embraces you with the same lusty life force that it graciously offered me. And remember, if it itches, play it.

CHICK COREA

A celebrated jazz pianist since the late 1960s, Anthony Armando "Chick" Corea grew up in the Boston area after World War II. The son of a bandleader, he began playing piano at the age of four, and was raised listening to musical influences including Beethoven, Chopin, and Mozart, alongside the recordings of Charlie Parker, Bud Powell, and Lester Young. Early in Corea's career, he developed a love for Latin American music. Today, he is best known for his free-floating improvisational style, and for tours ranging from fusion quintets to straight-ahead jazz quarters and trios to classical music.

I want to promote the idea of being an artist, and being a musician, because [it's] a very, very fulfilling life. It really is a kind of magical life, because we live on a planet that's not really conducive to what we do. It's not easy to go out and be creative; you have to survive. You have to make money, keep the body healthy, do all these various things.

But as artists and musicians, we've sort of played a trick on the rest of the world. [It] wants everybody to conform to the beat, to be a nine-to-fiver, to get up and do your job and not get too excited about anything, and just agree with everything that's going on. But in music and art, there's this little window that we've got that the whole planet agrees upon is a cool thing to do. It's all right to make music. It's all right to be yourself. In fact, the more yourself you are, the more money you make, I think, anyway.

Becoming a Responsible Citizen

George W. Bush

The forty-third president of the United States is a former governor of Texas, and only the second man in American history whose father was also president. Campaigning on a slogan of "compassionate conservatism," Bush has advocated policies based on the principles of limited government, personal responsibility, strong families, and local political control, but also has been criticized for a lack of environmental awareness, economic short-sightedness, and a unilateralist approach to foreign policy. Among his most potentially important, but as yet undeveloped notions, is that of amplifying citizen activism throughout community life.

Ultimately, your country is counting on each of you. Knute Rockne once said, "I have found that prayers work best when you have big players." We can pray for the justice of our country, but you're the big players we need to achieve it. Government can promote compassion, corporations and foundations can fund it, but the citizens—it's the citizens who provide it. A determined assault on poverty will require both an active government and active citizens.

There is more to citizenship than voting, though I urge you to do it. There is more to citizenship than paying taxes, though I'd strongly advise you to pay them. Citizenship is empty without concern for our fellow citizens, without the ties that bind us to one another and build a common good.

If you already realize this and you're acting on it, I thank you. If you haven't thought about it, I leave you with this challenge: serve a neighbor in need. Because a life of service is a life of significance. Because materialism, ultimately, is boring, and consumerism can build a prison of wants. Because a person who is not responsible for others is a person who is truly alone. Because there are few better ways to express our love for America than to care for other Americans. And because the same God who endows us with individual rights also calls us to social obligations.

Becoming a Writer

ERNEST HEMINGWAY

As one of America's greatest novelists, Ernest Hemingway produced such twentieth-century classics as *A Farewell to Arms, The Sun Also Rises,* and *For Whom the Bell Tolls.* While working as a journalist for the *Kansas City Star* before serving as a Red Cross volunteer during World War I, Hemingway developed the plain, forceful writing style that became his hallmark. As recounted by his son, physician Gregory Hemingway, in *Papa: A Personal Memoir,* the famed novelist offered this career advice:

I was eighteen, and Papa was paying for my food, lodging, and schooling. There were still times when we could talk and, strangely, Papa could still give good advice. I was in my last year of prep school, thinking about college, and about what would come next.

"It doesn't really matter what you do as long as you do something that really interests you, Gig," he said. "Something that you think is worthwhile and productive. And a lot of things are worthwhile, even though some narrow-minded bastards will say otherwise. And don't worry about money—if you're a failure at bird-watching, I'll support you! Have you thought much about what you'd really like to do?"

Actually, I had thought a lot . . . What I wanted to be was a Hemingway hero. But what the hell was it? I could analyze all his novels, but by far the simplest explanation was that a Hemingway hero was Hemingway himself, or the better parts of him. Still, to support yourself while doing all the exciting things that allowed you to exhibit grace under pressure, you had to be able to write about them. The passport to this glamorous life was talent, which was God-given, and a knowledge of the mechanics of writing, which could be taught. I decided to become a writer. I make light of it now, but I was dead serious then.

"Papa, what books influenced you most when you were a boy?" I asked him one vacation in Havana.

Papa seemed delighted by my question. He gave me a list of books to read, and my apprenticeship began.

Becoming an Artist

Nicholas Cage

Engaging, sleepy-eyed Nicholas Cage is among Hollywood's leading actors. A nephew of director Francis Ford Coppola, Cage grew up in Long Beach, California, and studied drama at the American Conservatory Theater in San Francisco. He graduated from teenage parts to a series of effective, idiosyncratic roles. Cage's best-known films include *Peggy Sue Got Married, Raising Arizona, Moonstruck, Leaving Las Vegas, The Rock, Family Man* and *Adaptation*.

That is what art does. You can heal yourself through art. You can cleanse your psyche and soul, and the result can, in turn, heal someone else because they can relate and feel that they are not alone.

What did we do before we had therapists? We listened to the piano player. We read great novels like Dostoyevsky's *Brothers Karamazov* and related to the situations the characters went through. Art can also just simply make you reflective or even happy for a few seconds, listening to an Elvis or Beatles song or Stravinsky on the radio. As artists, we keep the people of the world in a collective consciousness. We define ourselves in a relationship to the time we live in through art.

So how does one stay an artist? How do you protect your instrument? Elia Kazan once said that "Talent never dies. It can be discouraged, but it never dies." I've often thought that as actors, we are the instrument and when we fail, as we must, we will be criticized. It will be very painful, because you can't hide. You can't say, "My guitar was out of tune." You have to take the stone squarely on the chin and you have to ask yourself if you can handle it.

How badly do you want it? How hungry are you to be an artist and bare your soul to the world who may hate you for it? Are you willing to be publicly humiliated in the hopes that your peers may understand your art, or simply that you understand it? I think it's important that we all define success to ourselves as we embark on our life in art, and any reason is valid.

Do you want to become an artist because you want to be rich? Well, then make your choices based on that. Play it somewhat safely, don't [upset] too many people, and select work that will appeal to a lot of people.

Do you want to become an artist because you want to be famous? Well, you can do that a lot of different ways. You can become very famous, very quickly, by eating a cockroach in a movie. Do you want to be an artist because you want to meet girls and have them tear your clothes off? Make your choices based on that. Do you want to become an artist because you want to change the world in some way, any way at all?

They are all good reasons, but perhaps the best reason is because you can't help it, because it is inconceivable to you to do anything else, because without it you can't survive, because you could go crazy or broke or have no meaning in life.

I've always believed in treating my mind and body right, getting enough rest and exercise and fueling my imagination with the artistic achievements of others. But I also believe it's important to take chances in life. I believe the universe does away with that which sits on a fence; it destroys it because it has to make room for others. I don't ever want to sit idle in fear. I want to love and lose, if that's the way it has to be . . . I want to drive fast and eat and make love to remind me that I don't need to fear death. I want *experience* . . .

What you have learned at school is important, and you have achieved a remarkable honor. But experience is your teacher now.

Becoming an Enzyme for Change

PAM OMIDYAR

Pam and her husband Pierre Omidyar are the founders and chiefs of eBay, among the most successful Internet companies in the world. After studying molecular biology at Tufts University, she worked at an immunology laboratory. Later serving as management consultant to the pharmaceutical industry, Omidyar founded the HopeLab Foundation, a research institute devoted to improving the lives of young people coping with chronic illness. At present, she spends much of her time at California's Silicon Valley.

As someone who's loved biology for as long as I can remember, I've always been fascinated with the basic building blocks of life. But it wasn't until I got to Tufts and took biochemistry with Professor Feldberg that I realized: enzymes make really great role models!

As any biology major can tell you, enzymes are the catalysts that make possible biochemical reactions; enzymes increase the rate of a reaction, but are not themselves consumed by the reaction. To translate that into everyday English, enzymes are nature's activists.

Trying to imagine life without enzymes is an impossibility. Kind of like civil rights without Dr. King or Rosa Parks, or world peace without the moral courage of Jody Williams or the Dalai Lama. The world as we know it would not exist. And that really is the message we want to share with you today: Be an enzyme, a catalyst for change. Act on the environment around you. Make it your mission to make some small difference in the great scheme of life.

Becoming Successful in Business

John Johnson

John Johnson ranks among the most successful African Americans today in business. The entrepreneur is chairman and chief executive officer of the Johnson Publishing Company, which includes *Ebony, Jet,* and *Ebony Man.* Founded on a five-hundred-dollar loan from his mother in 1942 to start *Negro Digest,* the company also owns Fashion Fair Cosmetics, Ebony Cosmetics, and Supreme Beauty Products, and employs more than twenty-six hundred people. Johnson received a Distinguished Achievement Award in Journalism from the University of Southern California, and in 1989 published his autobiography.

I grew up in a segregated town, a city in Arkansas. It had only six hundred nineteen people when I was there. I went back fifty years later, and it still had six-hundred-and-something people. It did not have a high school, it had no running water, and blacks were relegated to the lowest possible level. But I always believed—and I got much of this belief from my mother—that if you prepared yourself, if you worked hard, and if you were patient, [success would follow]. I have received many honorary degrees, I have received many special ambassadorships, served on boards.

But I never got any of it when I thought I should have gotten it. So you've got to have patience.

Now that you've graduated from college, you think there are no more tests to take, that you won't have to take any more examinations. I need to tell you it's not true. I take an examination every day of my life.

My lawyer once said to me, "You're making decisions editorially, all day long, any one of which could put you out of business." So you really have to do things that you're afraid to do. If you're not doing things you're afraid to do, you're not really operating at your highest level. You have to dare.

I started my business many years ago with no money. But I thought I had a good idea. If you decide to go into business, you have to have a good idea. You can't go into a room, close the door, and come out with one. And you won't find it in any textbooks. You observe what is going on in the world. You look for opportunity to start something new. You go for a service that you can render better than anyone else. And then you have to go out and do it.

Becoming the Heroine of Your Life

NORA EPHRON

Beginning as a newspaper columnist for the *New York Post,* Nora Ephron became one of America's best-known journalists long before she wrote for the movies. She has directed such acclaimed films as *Sleepless in Seattle, Michael,* and *You've Got Mail,* and won an Academy Award screenplay nomination for *When Harry Met Sally,* one of the most highly regarded comedies in recent times. Other screenwriting credits include *Heartburn,* her own novel *Cookie,* and *My Blue Heaven.* She has been nominated three times for Academy Awards in the category of best original screenplay.

Above all, be the heroine of your life, not the victim. Because you don't have this alibi that my class had. This is one of the great achievements and mixed blessings you inherit: unlike us, you can't say nobody told you there were other options. Your education is a dress rehearsal for a life that is yours to lead. . . .

Yogi Berra, the former New York Yankee who made a specialty of saying things that were famously maladroit, quoted himself at a recent commencement speech he gave. "When you see a fork in the road," he said, "Take it."

Yes, it's supposed to be a joke, but . . . this is the life that many women lead: two paths diverge in a wood, and we get to take them both. It's another of the nicest things about being a women: we can do that.

Did I say it was hard? Yes, but let me say it again so that none of you can ever say the words, nobody said it was so hard. But it's also incredibly interesting. You are so lucky to have that life as an option.

Whatever you choose, however many roads you travel, I hope that you choose not to be a lady. I hope you find some way to break the rules and make a little trouble out there. And I also hope that you will choose to make some of that trouble on behalf of women. Thank you. Good luck. The first act of your life is over. Welcome to the best years of your lives.

Being Grateful for Good Times

Kurt Vonnegut

Kurt Vonnegut has been a popular American novelist for the past half century. Raised in Indianapolis and captured by the Nazis as a prisoner of war, he developed a unique blend of antiwar sentiment, social criticism, and science fiction in such acclaimed novels as *Slaughterhouse Five, Cat's Cradle, Welcome to the Monkey House,* and *God Bless You, Mr. Rosewater.* During the tumultuous Vietnam War era, Vonnegut was a literary icon on America's college campuses.

My Uncle Alex, my father's kid brother, [was] a Harvard graduate [and] was locally useful in Indianapolis as an honest insurance agent. He was also well read and wise.

One thing which Uncle Alex found objectionable about human beings was that they seldom took time out to notice when they were happy. He himself did his best to acknowledge it when times were sweet. We could be drinking lemonade in the shade of an apple tree in the summertime, and he would interrupt the conversation to say, "If this isn't nice, what is?"

So I hope that . . . you Adams and Eves in front of me will do the same for the rest of your lives. When things are going sweetly and peacefully, please pause a moment, and then say aloud, "If this isn't nice, what is?"

Be Prepared for Adversity

MARGARET ATWOOD

Margaret Atwood is among Canada's leading writers today. A novelist, poet, and critic, she grew up in Ottawa during the World War II era and was educated at the University of Toronto and Harvard. Her novels include *The Robber Bride, Cat's Eye, Surfacing,* and *The Handmaid's Tale,* which received the Governor General's Award in 1985. She has also edited two anthologies of Canadian poetry and short stories.

You are being launched—though ever since I experienced the process, I've wondered why "convocation" is the name for it. "Ejection" would be better. Even in the best of times, it's more or less like being pushed over a cliff, and these are not the best of times. In case you haven't figured it out already, I'm here to tell you that it's an armpit out there. As for your university degree, there are definitely going to be days when you will feel that you've been given a refrigerator and sent to the middle of a jungle, where there are no three-pronged grounded plugholes.

Not only that, the year will come when you will wake up in the middle of the night and realize the people you went to school with are in positions of power, and may soon actually be running things. If there's anything more calculated to thicken men's blood with cold, it's that. After all, you know how much they didn't know then, and, given yourself as an example, you can't assume they know a great deal more now.

You may feel that the only thing to do when you've reached this stage is to take up nail-biting, mantras, or jogging, all of which would be recognized by animal behavior specialists as substitution activities, like scratching, which are resorted to in moments of unresolved conflict.

Be Supportive of Dreams

GREG SMITH

Greg Smith is creator and host of *On a Roll,* the first nationally syndicated radio program about life from the perspective of Americans with disabilities. An African American, and the son of teachers, he grew up in Mississippi. Diagnosed with muscular dystrophy as a child, he became reliant on a motorized wheelchair by his early teens. Smith held several radio jobs, including hosting a football call-in show aired across the Southwest. Reflecting his growing interest in disability issues, he founded *On a Roll* in 1992.

I determined my own limitations. My parents always allowed me to discover what I could or could not do. . . . Think about your own issues, your own stand—that will make the world a better place—no matter what it is. I'm not just talking about disability issues. There are a multitude of opportunities all around us to improve the world we live in. If you can inspire one person and help make that person's dream more possible, maybe that person's dream can affect thousands, millions!

Seek your own dreams. And, at the same time, do everything you can to empower the people around you to achieve their dreams as well. If everyone would do just that, wouldn't the world be a better place?

Be True to Your Soul

ANNA QUINDLEN

Anna Quindlen, described earlier in this book, is both a prolific writer and lecturer. In this selection, she emphasizes to new graduates a key element of self-development.

Set aside what your friends expect, what your parents demand, what your acquaintances require. Set aside the messages this culture sends, through its advertising, its entertainment, its disdain and its disapproval, about how you should behave. . . .

This is the hard work of your life in the world: to make it all up as you go along, to acknowledge the introvert, the clown, the artist, the reserved, the distraught, the goofball, the thinker. . . .

Most commencement speeches suggest you take up something or other: the challenge of the future, a vision of the twenty-first century. Instead, I'd like you to give it up. Give up the backpack. Give up the nonsensical and punishing quest for perfection that dogs too many of us through too much of our lives. It is a quest that causes us to doubt and denigrate ourselves, our true selves, our quirks and foibles and great leaps into the unknown, and that is bad enough.

But this is worse: that someday, sometime, you will be somewhere, maybe on a day like today—a barn overlooking a pond in Vermont, the lip of the Grand Canyon at sunset. Maybe something bad will have happened: you will have lost someone you loved, or failed at something you wanted to succeed very much.

And sitting there, you will fall into the center of yourself. You will look for that core to sustain you. If you have been perfect all your life, and have managed to meet all the expectations of your family, your friends, your community, your society, chances are excellent that there will be a black hole where your core ought to be.

Don't take that chance. Begin to say "No" to the Greek chorus that thinks it knows the parameters of a happy life when all it knows is the homogenization of human experience. Listen to that small voice from inside you, that tells you to go another way. . . . And it will make all the difference in the world.

Be Willing to Take Chances

ALICE HOFFMAN

Raised on Long Island, Alice Hoffman wrote her first novel, *Property Of,* at the age of twenty-one, and was published shortly thereafter in 1974. Since then, Hoffman has authored more than a dozen books, including the best-sellers *The River King* and *Blue Diary*. Her novel *Practical Magic* was recently made into a movie starring Sandra Bullock and Nicole Kidman.

Although I'm not a scientist or a mathematician, I can give you the odds about one thing out in the real world, something I discovered on the day I walked away from one future [as a secretary] and began another [as a writer]: You have to take a chance. You have to do the thing you want to do, not the thing you're obligated to do. I'm not saying stop thinking about how you're going to pay your bills, I'm not saying ignore the future and live only in the present without a goal and a backup plan. But what I am saying is that what may appear to be the safe choice may be anything but. And what appears to be the risk—the impractical decision—the unattainable goal worthy of a dreamer or a fool, may in fact be your destiny.

Time and time again I have seen friends choose the safe course of action—the graduate school program that didn't speak to their hearts, the unexceptional job with a good pension and a great salary—only to have their safe choice fall to pieces. In the real world, businesses dissolve, government jobs get downgraded. If you go after safety, you may, after years of doing something you hate, wind up bankrupt anyway. But if you're true to yourself, there's no way you can lose. Even if you don't succeed completely, you might find another path you hadn't considered, and, more importantly, you won't have to live with the "should haves," the "might have beens," the "if onlys."

It's true that in the real world there are no guaranteed successes, no courses of action that will assuredly get you to where you want to go. But there is one guarantee: If you don't try, it will never happen. If you don't make an attempt, you're never going to get there. Don't judge yourself before you try, don't tell yourself what you want from your life is unattainable. . . . And [remember], sometimes the path you are meant to take is shown to you because you're good at something. Don't bypass something because it comes easily to you, because it's in your nature, because you enjoy something.

Bringing Democracy
Through Technology

BILL GATES

The richest man in the world, Bill Gates, is chairman and chief software architect for the Microsoft Corporation. It employs more than forty thousand people in sixty countries. The son of a wealthy Seattle attorney married to a schoolteacher, Gates was a precocious youngster who began programming computers at the age of thirteen. In 1973, he entered Harvard as a freshman, but left two years later to devote his energies to Microsoft, which he had founded with his childhood friend Paul Allen. Gates's books include *Business @ the Speed of Thought* and *The Road Ahead.* In recent years, Gates has turned increasingly to philanthropy and endowed the Bill and Melinda Gates Foundation with more than twenty-one billion dollars to support initiatives in global health and learning.

Fundamentally, technology makes it hard to control information, and I don't see any dilemma that we're facing. Nobody is coming to us [from the Chinese government] and saying, you know, put backdoors into software reports or anything like that. There's nothing like that. And there's almost a perfect correlation between the use of personal computer technology and how democratic a society is, and in fact, I'm very optimistic about China because right now you're seeing this huge rise in the personal computer.

There may be some substantial lag time on the order of a decade, but the kind of developments that are taking place there and the kind of empowerment that comes out of that will lead over time to more political choices probably in a smooth evolutionary way.

So I think everybody in the technology industry can feel good about that, and there's nothing pushing back the other way. There's nothing where somebody is saying, "Build this thing in a way that prevents information from being shared."

Bringing Psychology to the World

Edward Hoffman

As a licensed psychologist based in New York City, I have authored more than a dozen books on topics including fatherhood, romantic compatibility, and biographies of psychological founders. These include *The Drive for Self: Alfred Adler and the Founding of Individual Psychology*, which won a 1996 Gradiva Award. Alongside his colleagues Sigmund Freud and Carl Jung, Adler is credited with building the modern fields of personality study and psychotherapy.

As Alfred Adler's biographer, I have learned many valuable lessons in studying his life. The four years I spent on this project decisively showed me that Adler achieved his great influence on modern psychology, child guidance, and education by the force of his own personality—and that, to whatever extent possible, we can apply these lessons, too. Today, as you receive your degrees to become professional counselors and clinicians, I'd like to highlight five specific elements vital to Adler's success:

1. He was optimistic by nature. American journalists admiringly described him in the 1920s as "bubbling with enthusiasm" and "a dynamo of optimism." Of course, Adler as a practicing and

perceptive medical psychologist saw the darker side of human nature, motivations, and goals. But he never let that awareness impede his effort to make the world a more hospitable place, both in families and schools, for growing children. He was able to integrate his view of the "dark side" into a broader, more inclusive, and realistic optimism about human accomplishment.

2. He made his message clear and down-to-earth, avoiding scientific jargon, and instead using examples familiar to everyone in daily life. Adler knew that to overcome long-standing prejudices about child-rearing and education, he had to be exciting and even dramatic as a speaker. To help change authoritarian attitudes—in his day, most teachers and parents, for example, thought that hitting children was a perfectly acceptable form of discipline—Adler projected a warm and witty style. Gentle humor, he found, is a far more effective way to open people up to new ideas than heavy-handed sermonizing.

3. He was willing, even eager, to "talk psychology" with persons from many different backgrounds, not only professionals in mental health, social science, or education. To look at Adler's lecture schedule in his final years—when he was already in his midsixties—is to be truly impressed, for he often gave several different lectures *on the same day* to varied groups of parents, teachers, as well as the general public. Unlike his more aloof colleagues like Sigmund Freud

and Carl Jung, Adler believed in "democratizing psychology"—that is, sharing its scientific insights with virtually everyone who was willing to listen, be open, and change for the better. For only by taking psychology's teachings to the masses of men and women could a more harmonious world be achieved, he believed.

4. He kept growing intellectually, refusing to rest on laurels and past accomplishments. To those who knew Adler well, he was a marvel of personal energy—but more importantly, that energy was spent on continually learning new matters about children, families, and community. Right up until his death, his succession of books provided exciting new insights, rather than a rehash of previously expressed ideas. Equally significant, although Adler was already acclaimed throughout Europe by middle age, he taught himself to speak English effectively, so that he could lecture throughout the United States and other English-speaking countries. He gave his first such lectures in his midfifties, making memorable mistakes in grammar, but soon enough, the mistakes disappeared and his fresh approach to understanding children enthralled new audiences from New York to California and many places in between.

5. Finally, Adler always kept the "big picture" in mind, and that is what made him a true visionary and leader. Over the course of his long career that saw many triumphs and achievements, but also witnessed the rise of European fascism and Nazism that

destroyed much of his humanistic efforts in education, Adler always viewed his work in large historical terms. Late in life, he told his friends that whether his name would even be remembered in psychology's history was not so important—what mattered far more was that his progressive approach to child development, parenting, and education become accepted. And in this respect, as you graduates today know well, Adler certainly achieved his goal.

As you become helpers in a world that still needs psychology's evolving insights and therapeutic methods, Adler's inspiring life is a beacon to us all.

Building on Your Learning

ELIE WIESEL

Elie Wiesel is probably the world's most respected and influential Holocaust survivor and spokesperson. Born into a religious Jewish Romanian family in the village of Sighet, Wiesel was sixteen years old when deported, along with his entire family and all his Jewish neighbors, to the Auschwitz death camp. His parents and younger sister Tsipouka were killed, but young Wiesel was forced into slave labor at Buchenwald, another German death camp. After World War II ended, he settled in France, where he studied at the Sorbonne and became a journalist. In 1956, he relocated to the United States and acquired citizenship.

Wiesel's first novel, *Night*, chronicled his experiences at the hands of the Nazis, and was followed by works including *Dawn, The Town Beyond the Wall, A Beggar in Jerusalem*, and many others. In 1985, Wiesel was awarded the U.S. Congressional Gold Medal of Achievement, and the following year he won the Nobel Peace Prize. Traveling frequently around the globe as a lecturer, Wiesel holds a professorship at Boston University. These words convey his sense of what education is all about:

From now on, no more exams, no more apprehension. Still, I hope you will not stop being students. The fact that you will not have exams does not mean that you should not go on learning. You must continue to listen to Plato, or to Jeremiah, or both; you must continue to come closer to other fellow human beings, just as you have been closer here among yourselves or with your fine, inspiring teachers.

What do you take from here? A story, a formula, maybe a hand-shake, a special encounter, a friendship. What will remain except a diploma? Much must remain because when two persons meet, a mystery is born. Take that mystery and respect it, and if possible, invest it with more meaning, with more miraculous significance.

Cherishing Your Loved Ones

JONATHAN KOZOL

For more than thirty years, Jonathan Kozol has written and lectured about children's education, poverty, and related issues. Kozol's first work of nonfiction, *Death at an Early Age,* based on his own teaching experience in a Boston slum, won a National Book Award in 1968. His many other books include *Choosing Excellence, Illiterate America,* and most recently, *Amazing Grace,* which addressed the issue of race and poverty in the South Bronx.

I'm at an age when time increasingly seems precious. Many of the people I love most in this life have gone now from the earth. Others who are in the forefront of the fight for decent education for our children have retired. My beloved friend, the sweetest man I've ever known, Fred Rogers, has retired—Mr. Rogers. . . . My own mother is ninety-eight years old [and] lives right here in Boston. My mother's lived nearly a century. I look into her eyes sometimes and think, "My God, she was a little girl in junior high school when the Red Sox won their last World Series."

She helped me so much when I was a young man in the civil rights campaigns. She came out on the picket lines with the black leaders of

Boston and marched with us and sang the song "Seven," though she didn't know the words. She helped me then, helps me still, scolds me still. To be honest, I can't bear the thought of losing her. I pray like a child that she'll live forever, but of course, I know she can't. None of us can. We all know we will die and lose the ones we love the most to death.

The old trees and the playfulness of children will outlive us all. My friends, life goes so fast. Use it well. God bless.

Choosing the Right Work

David Halberstam

A prominent journalistic jack-of-all-trades for decades, David Halberstam has been a war correspondent as well as a prolific writer for newspapers and magazines on American politics, foreign policy decision-making, social history, and sports including baseball, basketball, and rowing. His most influential book is undoubtedly *The Best and the Brightest,* a searing analysis of how the United States bungled its way in the Vietnam War. Among Halberstam's other books are *October 1964, The Fifties, Playing for Keeps,* and *Summer of 49.*

Other than the choice of a lifetime partner, nothing determines happiness so much as choosing the right kind of work. It is a choice about what's good for you, not what's good for others whom you greatly respect, your parents, an admired professor, your friends, a significant other whom you suspect may be dazzled by a greater or loftier choice of profession. The choice is not about what makes them happy, but what makes you happy. Not what seems to show that you are successful by the exterior standards of the society. Not what brings you the biggest salary—particularly in the beginning when those things seem so important—and the biggest house, or the greatest respect from Wall Street, but what makes you feel complete and happy and makes you feel, for this is no small thing, like part of something larger than yourself. . . .

Don't be afraid to make some mistakes when you are young. Do not be afraid to try and fail early in your life. We often stumble toward the things we will end up doing best; do not be afraid to take chances when you are young, to choose the unconventional over the conventional. Often it is the experience in the unconventional which prepares you best for the conventional. Be aware that it's all right to make mistakes, and it is all right to make mistakes and fail. The price of failure when you are young is much lower than when you are older. . . .

To choose the right profession is very hard. First you have to choose the right profession—and then you have to work very hard for the rest of your lives to sustain the thing you happen to love. As the noted philosopher, basketball player, and sports commentator, Julius Erving—Dr. J to the Laker fans here—once said, "Being a professional is doing the things you love to do on the days when you don't feel like doing them."

Confronting Your Graduation Photo

DAVE BARRY

Dave Barry, a syndicated columnist for the Miami Herald, *is widely read for such humorous books as* Dave Barry Slept Here, Claw Your Way to the Top, *and* Dave Barry's Guide to Marriage and/or Sex. *Raised in suburban New York City, he decided on a journalism career, and first gained wide popularity in the early 1980s for his satirical articles on contemporary family life and other topics.* In Dave Barry Is Not Making This Up, *he turned his wit to this facet of graduation:*

Yes, young people, modern technology promises an exciting future. But you must also learn from the wisdom of your elders, and if there is one piece of advice that I would offer you, it is this: Burn your yearbook right now. Because otherwise, years from now, feeling nostalgic, you'll open it up to your photo, and this alien *geek* will be staring out at you, and your children will beg you to tell them that they're adopted.

It is a known scientific fact that, no matter how good your yearbook photo looks now, after fifteen years of being pressed up against somebody else's face in the dark and mysterious yearbook environment, it will transmute itself into a humiliating picture of a total goober. This is true of everybody.

Creating a Meaningful Life

EDWARD I. KOCH

Best known for his "How'm I doing?" approach to politics and life, Edward Koch served as New York City's mayor for twelve tumultuous years. Since leaving public office in 1989, he has remained highly active as a popular radio talk-show host, newspaper columnist, and a highly placed Manhattan attorney.

Koch grew up in New York City and Newark in the 1920s and '30s. He liked to joke in later years that he had "moved from one slum to another." His father, Louis, struggled as a Polish-Jewish immigrant, and during the Depression his small business as a furrier shut down permanently. Edward Koch has viewed adversity as among life's challenges:

Let me begin with a bit of advice . . . that will serve you better than anything anyone could say to you at this time. If you are unhappy in your career choice after giving it a fair shake, quit. Leave it and look for an opportunity that will make you happy. Remember, you will spend at least a third of your life at work. No matter how well a job pays, if it is drudgery, it isn't worth it. Don't wait. Make your decision before financial and family obligations make it too difficult to leave.

I always tried to follow that advice myself. As a lawyer, I could have had a number of different careers. But I loved politics, and that's how I ended up in City Hall. Even in politics, I have always tried to follow my own instincts.

Creating Joy

GOLDIE HAWN

Goldie Hawn's acting career has spanned more than thirty years. Most recently starring in *The Banger Sisters* and *The Out-of-Towners,* her best-known roles include *First Wives Club* and *Private Benjamin.* Raised in Washington, D.C., she launched her TV career in comedy roles with the *Rowan & Martin Laugh-In* series.

On this special day, if I had one gift to give you, all it would be is a life filled with happiness and joy. Oh, I don't mean that life should always be happy, no. We know that's not possible, but my hope is that you all could cultivate a "joy muscle" so you can use it to "lift you back to yourselves" in times of sadness, stress, and disappointment. It's not a frivolous thing to aspire to live a joyful life. It takes work . . . Focus . . . Intention. And knowing yourself!

A wish to have a happy heart is the beginning. Just to wish. I know that right now, some of your heads are spinning with questions. Big questions like:

What I am going to do?

How will I make money?

How will I succeed?

How will I live up to others' expectations of me, including my own?

Jeez, stop! Our twenties are the years to plant, to nurture yourself in preparation for the future, so when you reach life's inevitable, you have the grounding to handle the tasks in front of you. Think of this time as a ladder of discovery into the truth of your own special being.

Find out who you are, what you think, learn to listen to the sounds of your own heart. Please don't pound your head against those imaginary walls in hopes to become something right away. No, not yet!

Lift your head to the sky and bay at the moon. See the world. Keep your mind open to new ideas and adventure out of your circle of expectations, listen to the wisdom of elders and travel to destinations without a map. The people you meet along the way may thrill you with their precious time and assistance—and perhaps keep a fire under your love of humankind.

Cultivate Experience

RALPH WALDO EMERSON

A revered figure in nineteenth-century American philosophy, Ralph Waldo Emerson inspired numerous writers and thinkers, including Emily Dickinson, Herman Melville, Henry James, and his close friend Henry David Thoreau. Originally a Unitarian minister, in the 1830s Emerson became immensely successful as an independent writer and lecturer. His key themes included self-reliance, individuality, and reverence for nature. A doting father to his four children and speaking often in college settings, Emerson had inspirational goals for youth:

This world—this shadow of the soul, or *other me*—lies wide around. Its attractions are the keys which unlock my thoughts and make me acquainted with myself. I run eagerly into this resounding tumult. I grasp the hands of those next to me, and take my place in the ring to suffer and to work, taught by an instinct that so shall the dumb abyss be vocal with speech. I pierce its order; I dissipate its fear; I dispose of it within the circuit of my expanding life.

So much only of life as I know by experience, so much of the wilderness have I vanquished and planted, or so far have I extended my being, my dominion. I do not see how any man can afford, for the sake of his nerves and his nap, to spare any action in which he can partake. It is pearls and rubies to his discourse. Drudgery, calamity, exasperation, want, are instructors in eloquence and wisdom.

Cultivate Reading

George Will

George Will is an ABC News commentator, Pulitzer Prize winner, and author of a syndicated column that appears in more than four hundred fifty newspapers. He became a contributing editor of *Newsweek* in 1976, and one year later was awarded the Pulitzer Prize for Commentary. His books include *The Pursuit of Happiness and Other Sobering Thoughts, Leveling Wind,* and *Men at Work: The Craft of Baseball.*

A common cultural vocabulary is more than just, in Thomas Burke's phrase, "the decent drapery of life." It is more than merely decorative. It is practical, because it facilitates adult conversation. As has been said, societies should be like icebergs: "Beneath the surface, there's the unseen seven-eighths, the shared history on which the top eighth sits." Unfortunately, the bottom seven-eighths is melting because "a modern, electronic culture exists in a state of perpetual anticipation. . . ."

I write for newspapers; I work on television. But this I know: Books remain the best, the primary carrier of ideas. And history is the history of mind. It is, not only because ideas have consequences, but because only ideas have large and lasting consequences.

Ours is a proudly practical society that prefers people of "action" to people of mere contemplation. But the rise—the inundating rise—of graphic journalism and entertainment has at least served to remind us of a basic fact: Reading is an activity [that] must be encouraged, not merely by being required, but [also by] being honored.

Cultivate Your Friendships

BILLIE JEAN KING

Raised in southern California, Billie Jean King was an exceptional softball player in her early years. Yet she knew that no significant future existed for a woman in softball. Her parents introduced her to tennis, the game that would change her life and those of other women. In 1967, she was selected as Outstanding Female Athlete of the World, in 1972 she was named *Sports Illustrated* Sportsperson of the Year—the first woman to be so honored—and in 1973 she was dubbed Female Athlete of the Year. Billie Jean King established the first successful women's professional tennis tour, founded tennis clinics for underprivileged children, and has continued to speak out for women and their right to earn comparable money in tennis and other sports. Her constant lobbying and commitments have helped to break many barriers for women.

As you leave today, to go on, I don't want you to forget your friendships. Your friendships, your relationships, your networking, and your mentoring. If it hadn't been for a friend, I would have never played tennis. It was the last sport I ever played. I played every other sport before I played tennis. All team sports. Always a team sport. And a friend of mine, Susan Williams, in the fifth grade said, "Do you want to play tennis?" And I said, "What's tennis?"

So my friend Susan Williams brought me to play tennis, and at my first free lesson at the public park, I decided I wanted to be the number one tennis player in the world. But if it hadn't been for Susan, I wouldn't have gotten there.

So don't lose your friendships and your acquaintances that you have here today. Don't ever lose them. They'll be a part of your networking as you get older. It'll be important.

Cultivating Civility

DONNA SHALALA

Serving for eight years as U.S. secretary of health and human services in the Clinton administration, Donna Shalala had earlier earned recognition as president of New York City's Hunter College and chancellor of the University of Wisconsin at Madison. Raised in Cleveland, she taught political science at several universities. In 1975, while still teaching, Shalala served as director and treasurer of the Municipal Assistance Corporation, credited with helping rescue New York City from near bankruptcy. Seeking to revise the financial structure of America's health care system has been among her leading goals.

When I was at Syracuse University, the snowball fights were world class. My diet consisted mostly of pizza. I had very little sleep. I developed a lifelong skepticism of anyone in charge. And it was here—a place of discussion and dialogue, energy and excitement—that I was intellectually disciplined by outstanding teachers and scholars.

Being back at Syracuse reminds me a little bit of the story about George Bernard Shaw and Winston Churchill. You see, Shaw had a big play opening up, and he sent Churchill two tickets with a searing note that read: "Bring a friend—*if you have one.*"

Churchill fired back a letter saying, "Sorry, I can't make it opening night. Send me tickets to the second night's show—*if there is one!*"

In that spirit, I thank you for bringing me back to Syracuse. Your graduation comes at a critical juncture in our nation's history. How ironic, that at a time when the Cold War has ended and democracy is replacing totalitarianism throughout the world, we see the fault lines of division rippling through our country. No matter what your political beliefs, all of us can agree that political debate has become too polarized. Antipathy has replaced empathy. Division has replaced discourse. And simplistic solutions have replaced thoughtful answers.

Part of your inheritance and part of your new responsibility will be to reignite the American values of civility and consensus, and renew the American tradition of finding pragmatic solutions to our greatest challenges.

Discovering Who You Are

RAY BRADBURY

Ray Bradbury ranks among the greatest science-fiction writers of our time. Though his formal schooling ended with high school, he has written more than forty books, including *Fahrenheit 451, The Martian Chronicles, The Illustrated Man, I Sing the Body Electric,* and *Quicker Than the Eye*. After achieving fame as a science-fiction novelist, Bradbury has also devoted time to screenplays, radio dramas, essays, and poems. His work has won innumerable awards including the O. Henry Memorial Award, and been adapted for film and television.

Now, why are you here? You've been put here because the universe exists. There's no use to the universe existing if there isn't someone there to see it. Your job is to see it. Your job is to witness. To witness, to understand, to comprehend, and to celebrate! To celebrate with your lives. At the end of your life, if you didn't come to that end, and look back and realize that you did not celebrate, then you wasted it.

Your function is God-given. To act on your genetics, to be what you were born to be—find out what it is, and do it. The Armenians have a saying: that in the hour of your birth, God thumbprints thee with a genetic thumbprint in the middle of your forehead. But in the hour of your birth, that thumbprint vanishes back into your flesh. Your job, as young people, is to look into the mirror every day of your life, and see the shape of that genetic thumbprint, and find out just who in the hell you are. It's a big job, but a wonderful job.

Don't Be a Loser

LARRY ELLISON

Chief executive officer of the Oracle Corporation since 1977, Larry Ellison has been ranked among America's richest men and women. A college dropout who is renowned as a tough-talking risk-taker with superb business instincts, Ellison has been a board member of Apple Computer and the recipient of many honors and awards including Entrepreneur of the Year from the Harvard School of Business. A sailboat racer and jet pilot with lavish tastes, Ellison has prided himself on flouting convention when it comes to courting and counseling success.

Please take a good look around you. Look at the classmate on your left. Look at the classmate on your right. Now, consider this: five years from now, ten years from now, even thirty years from now, odds are the person on your left is going to be a loser. The person on your right, meanwhile, will also be a loser. And you, in the middle? What can you expect? Loser. Loserhood. *Loser Cum Laude.*

In fact, as I look out before me today, I don't see a thousand hopes for a bright tomorrow. I don't see a thousand future leaders in a thousand industries. I see a thousand losers.

You're upset. That's understandable. After all, how can I, Lawrence "Larry" Ellison, college dropout, have the audacity to spout such heresy to the graduating class of one of the nation's most prestigious institutions? I'll tell you why. Because I, Lawrence "Larry" Ellison, second richest man on the planet, am a college dropout, and you are not.

Because Bill Gates, richest man on the planet—for now, anyway—is a college dropout, and you are not.

Because Paul Allen, the third richest man on the planet, dropped out of college, and you did not.

And for good measure, because Michael Dell, Number Nine on the list and moving up fast, is a college dropout, and you, yet again, are not.

Hmmmmm, you're very upset. That's understandable. So let me stroke your egos for a moment by pointing out, quite sincerely, that your diplomas were not earned in vain. Most of you, I imagine, have spent four to five years here, and in many ways, what you've learned and endured will serve you well in the years ahead. You've established good work habits. You've established a network of people that will help you down the road. And you've established what will be lifelong relationships with the word "therapy." All of that is good.

For in truth, you will need that network. You will need that therapy. You will need them because you didn't drop out, and so you will never be among the richest people in the world.

Envision a Life That You Love

SUZAN-LORI PARKS

Suzan-Lori Parks is a well-known playwright who teaches as writer-in-residence at the New School for Social Research. Her early short plays include *Betting on the Dust Commander, Fishes,* and *Imperceptible Mutabilities in the Third Kingdom,* which won the Obie Award for the best off-Broadway play in 1990. The daughter of an army officer, Parks traveled widely as a child and studied writing with James Baldwin. After that experience, she went to London for a year to study acting. Among her recent plays are *In the Blood,* which depicts the life of a homeless, single mother, and *Topdog/Underdog,* for which she won the Pulitzer Prize.

As you walk your road, as you live your life, relish the road. And relish the fact that the road of your life will probably be a winding road. Something like the yellow brick road in *The Wizard of Oz.* You see the glory of Oz up ahead, but there are lots of twists and turns along the way—lots of tin men, lots of green women . . .

Be bold. Envision yourself living a life that you love. Believe, even if you can only muster your faith for just this moment—believe that the sort of life you wish to live is, at this very moment, just waiting for you to summon it up. And when you wish it, you begin moving toward it, and it, in turn, begins moving toward you.

Expanding Your Possibilities

BILL CLINTON

The charismatic forty-second president of the United States left a domestic and internationalist legacy still much too new to be appraised in an accurate long-term perspective. But indisputably, he was admired around the world more than any other U.S. president in modern times since Kennedy. Though how much credit his administration can justifiably take remains a moot point, the Clinton years marked an almost historically unprecedented of American economic expansion and opportunity.

Our mission today must be to ensure that all of our people have the opportunity to live out their dreams in a nation that remains the world's strongest force for peace and freedom, for prosperity, for our commitment that we can respect our diversity and still find unity.

This is about more than money. Opportunity is what defines this country. For two hundred twenty years, the idea of opportunity for all and the freedom to seize it have literally been the defining elements of America. They were always ideals, never perfectly realized, but always our history has been a steady march of striving to live up to them.

Having these ideals achievable, imaginable for all is an important part of maintaining our sense of democracy and our ability to forge an American community with such disparate elements of race and religion and ethnicity across so many borders that could so easily divide this country.

And so I say to you, creating opportunity for all, the opportunity that everyone has that many of you are now exercising, dreaming about your future, that is what you must do to make sure that this Age of Possibility is really that for all Americans.

Expecting the Unexpected

John Grisham

John Grisham is among the world's most popular writers. His legal thrillers, many of which have been made into movies, include *The Firm, The Chamber, The Client, The Pelican Brief, The Gingerbread Man,* and *The Rainmaker.* Grisham earned his law degree from the University of Mississippi and served seven years as a state legislator before *The Firm*'s huge success in 1988 catapulted his writing career. Grisham's recent novels have included *The Partner, The Testament,* and *The Brethren.*

When I sat out there fifteen years ago, I was rather smug and confident, perhaps even a bit arrogant because I, at the age of twenty-two, had already figured out my life. I had it all planned, and was certain things would fall neatly into place. . . . Fifteen years ago, I had it all planned, and thank goodness it didn't work out.

If you're sitting out there now with a nice, neat little outline for the next ten years, you'd better be careful. Life may have other plans. Life will present you with unexpected opportunities, and it will be up to you to take a chance, to be bold, to have faith, and go for it. Life will also present you with bad luck and hardship, and maybe even tragedy, so get ready for it. It happens to everyone.

Finding Your Courage

RUDOLPH GIULIANI

Capping a long career in public service and two successful terms as mayor in which he helped make New York City considerably more livable to its residents, Giuliani is undoubtedly best known for his inspirational leadership during the weeks that followed the horror of September 11, 2001. With a calmly determined, assured, and almost ministerial manner that seemed little evidenced before the terrorist destruction of the World Trade Center, Giuliani gave virtually all New Yorkers, Americans, and indeed much of the outraged world a potent sense of hope and courage.

When you think of courage, don't think of a lack of fear. Courage is about being afraid, but being able to do what you have to do, anyway. Courage is about seeing those flames [at the burning World Trade Center], knowing the fear, knowing you're going into the worst fire you'd ever face in your entire life, and knowing you may never return. . . .

That's what courage is about, it's about managing your fears. Please remember that. You're going to have to do it all your life. I have to do it, you have to do it. If you want to succeed, if you want to be happy, if you want to lead, you have to manage your fears. Don't ever think it's about the lack of fear. It's about managing your fears.

Finding Your Passion

AHMET ERTEGUN

Ahmet Ertegun has been a leading producer of American pop music for nearly a half century. Creating the Cat record label in 1954 and Atlas Records the year after, the Turkish-born Ertegun joined Atlantic Records in 1956 and steadily built its album department into an industrial powerhouse, best known for its jazz and rhythm-and-blues performers including John Coltrane, Charles Mingus, Ornette Coleman, the Modern Jazz Quartet, and later, Ray Charles, the Drifters, Arethra Franklin, Wilson Pickett, and Roberta Flack. In the 1970s, he produced rock acts such as Dr. John, Led Zeppelin, and Dire Straits. Though less directly involved today as a producer, Ertegun still serves as chairman of Atlantic Records.

There are people that love nothing passionately. They get into whatever makes them the most money. And they get to love it for the sake of that goal. There are those who have to take whatever opportunity they get just for survival. The person who loves the theater but works as a clerk has a very different quality of life than a person who loves literature and teaches it at a university, or is a book editor or a literary critic.

So if you do have a love, try to pursue that. Because then work is no longer work. But it is what you enjoy doing the most. Your goal does not have to be grand or grandiose. But it has to be something that you dedicate yourself to.

DAVID KELLEY

A former Boston lawyer, David Kelley switched careers to become a Hollywood screenwriter and producer. His first success came with *L.A. Law,* which arose partly from personal experience in the legal field. Kelley's subsequent successful TV projects have included *Ally McBeal, Doogie Howser, M.D.,* and *Boston Public.* Now part of the production division of Twentieth Century Fox, Kelley is married to actress Michelle Pfeiffer.

Decide not what you want to *be,* but what you want to *do.* Again, that sounds very simple, but the majority of you will go to work doing not really what you want to do, in the hopes of becoming what you want to be. The true reward for doing is the opportunity to do more.

Love what you do, or move on. Franz Kafka once said, "The meaning of life is that it stops." And it's true, so don't waste it. Love your [work].

CHARLIE ROSE

Admired as one of America's premier interviewers is Emmy Award–winning Charlie Rose. Well known as the genial host of *Charlie Rose,* the nightly PBS show, he engages leading thinkers, writers, scientists, entertainers, and newsmakers in lively, intelligent dialogue. Also a correspondent for *60 Minutes II,* the CBS news program, the North Carolina–born Rose holds a law degree from Duke University and has garnered many broadcasting awards.

I spoke to Bill Gates on Thursday of this past week. We had a hamburger at a hamburger place that he goes to. I paid. He's got a hundred billion and I've got much less, but we talked about Harvard where he went to college—and where he dropped out. He was a student who fell in love with computers and he saw their potential and he left Harvard, I am sure to his parents' dismay, in order to follow his instincts.

He had a dream that he could put computers on every desk and in every home, and now he has—because he took a chance. [He has] the resources and, I believe, the ambition, to change the world for the better not by creating new software alone, but also by giving away money for new vaccines to fight diseases. He is not a billboard for not getting a degree; he is a billboard for following your instincts and taking your heart where it wants to go.

Finding Your Sacred Calling

OPRAH WINFREY

"Oprah Winfrey arguably has more influence on the culture than any university president, politician, or religious leader, except perhaps the Pope," asserted *Vanity Fair*. As host of the Chicago-based *Oprah Winfrey Show* since 1985, Oprah has won more than thirty Daytime Emmys and emerged from an impoverished, out-of-wedlock background to become one of America's richest women; she joins Mary Pickford and Lucille Ball as the only women to own their own movie production studios. Oprah earned a Golden Globe and an Academy Award nomination for her inspiring performance in the racially oriented film *The Color Purple*.

There is a sacred calling on each of our lives that goes beyond this degree that you're about to receive. There is a sacred contract that you made—that I made—with the Creator, when we came into being. Not just the sperm and egg meeting when we came into the essence of who we were created to be. You made a contract, you had a calling. And whether you know it or not, it is your job to find out what that calling is, and get about the business of doing it.

The force divine—God—can dream a bigger dream for you than you can dream for yourself. Surrender to that dream, the universe's dream for yourself.

When you decide that your life will be different, that your circumstances will be different, that your environment will be different—when you decide—that is when it changes. You give yourself the authority to be who you were meant to be. You continue to evolve your life through every thought, through every feeling, and every action. That is how we are most created equal.

Things aren't just happening to any of us. So, as you get the degree, be aware of that calling. Be aware of what you're calling in, and calling up, and calling out of yourself—and everybody else you encounter. Be aware, and honor that calling.

Fostering Excellence

Tony Bennett

Tony Bennett (Anthony Benedetto) is among America's most admired pop vocalists for songs that include "The Beat of My Heart," "Blue Velvet," and "I Left My Heart in San Francisco." Growing up in 1930s New York City as the son of Italian immigrants who owned a grocery, he decided during his teens on a singing career. Then at the age of eighteen, he was drafted into the U.S. Army and saw combat in Europe during World War II. By the late 1940s, Bennett had acquired a manager and got his big break when Bob Hope saw him perform. Today Bennett seems like the last of a breed, but remains as popular as ever.

My great friend, my greatest friend, was Frank Sinatra. When I first started to sing, I had no idea [what I was doing]. I was very nervous. I said to him, "How do I handle my nervousness?" He said, "Don't worry about it. The audience doesn't mind if you're nervous—it's when you're not nervous. If you don't care, they're not going to care. So if you're nervous, they're going to help you out."

He also said to me, "Don't ever do [silly songs]. A lot of marketers and producers will tell you to sing silly songs because they just want to make a lot of money. Just stay with great songs, with the most intelligent."

We have a great tradition in America. We're so young, we don't even realize that in the golden era in the 1930s and '40s we had Cole Porter, Irving Berlin, Jerome Kern, Harold Arlen, George and Ira Gershwin. Where is there a George and Ira Gershwin today?

These are the beautiful songs that will live thousands of years from now and show everybody in the world what a great country we had, that we invented American popular music. Those songs never die. The marketing people will tell you they're old songs. They're not old songs, they're great songs. They're written so well, [by those who] studied Shakespeare, haiku poetry, Gilbert and Sullivan. They studied every form of writer from Shakespeare on down, and that's why they became great songwriters. . . .

When you go out into the world, you'll find out that they say, "We don't do that anymore. That's old-fashioned." But don't let them fool you. Stay with all the integrity you can muster up and stay with it, and in a very good psychological way, fight for your life and become very successful.

Gaining a Global Awareness

Richard Nixon

The thirty-seventh president of the United States was a cogent internationalist who drew on his two vice-presidential terms under Eisenhower from 1953 to 1961 in building such notable achievements as opening relations with China and significantly reducing military tensions with the Soviet Union. After resigning from office in disgrace during the Watergate scandal in 1974, the reclusive Nixon developed a new career as a writer whose lucid and well-received books on foreign policy included *Real Peace, No More Vietnams, Victory Without War,* and *Seize the Moment: America's Challenges in a One-Superpower World.*

Our foreign policy must reflect our ideals, and it must reflect our purposes. We can never, as Americans, acquiesce in the suppression of human liberties. We must do all that we reasonably can to promote justice, and for this reason, we continue to adhere firmly to certain humane principles, not only in appropriate international forums, but also in our private exchanges with other governments—where this can be effective. But we must recognize that we are more faithful to our ideals by being concerned with results, and we achieve more results through diplomatic action than through hundreds of eloquent speeches.

But there are limits to what we can do, and we must ask ourselves some very hard questions, questions which I know members of this class have asked themselves many times. What is our capability to change the domestic structure of other nations? Would a slowdown or reversal of détente help or hurt the positive evolution of other social systems? What price—in terms of renewed conflict—are we willing to pay to bring pressure to bear for humane causes? . . .

The concepts of national security, partnership, negotiation with adversaries are the central pillars of the "structure of peace" this administration has outlined as its objective.

GERALD FORD

As vice president, Gerald Ford became the thirty-eighth U.S. president when Richard Nixon resigned from office in 1974. Pardoning Nixon in advance from all possible criminal charges resulting from his Watergate cover-up actions was undoubtedly Ford's most difficult political decision, and probably cost him the presidency. During his administration, Ford continued the policy of military détente with the Soviet Union, forged the Helsinki accords on human rights, made personal visits to Japan and China, and co-sponsored the first international economic summit meeting.

I want to tell the world: Let's grow food together, but let's also learn more about nutrition, about weather forecasting, about irrigation, about the many other specialties involved in helping people to help themselves.

We must learn more about people, about the development of communities, architecture, engineering, education, motivation, productivity, public health and medicine, political, legal, and social organization. All of these specialties, and many, many more are required if young people like you are to help this nation develop an agenda for the future—your future, our country's future.

Gaining Self-Respect

GEORGE MITCHELL

Respected former U.S. senator George Mitchell helped Northern Ireland reach an historic peace agreement after he served as moderator in twenty-two months of talks. Although considered a bland politician, Mitchell has blossomed as a mediator.

When you take the bar exam, make sure you don't do what the young Irish student did when he took it in early December. Frustrated by the difficulty of the questions, he wrote on the last one, "God alone knows the answer to this question. Merry Christmas." When he got the paper back, there was this response: "God gets an A, you fail. Happy New Year."

For most human beings, life is in essence a never-ending search for respect. First and foremost, self-respect, then the respect of others. There are many ways to achieve respect, but for me, none is more certain and rewarding than service to others. . . . Real fulfillment in your life will come from striving with all of your physical and spiritual might for a worthwhile objective that helps others and is larger than your self-interest.

Get to Know Many People

Eleanor Roosevelt was respected not merely as the wife of President Franklin D. Roosevelt during America's darkest period, but also as a distinguished public figure in her own right. She was probably the most active first lady in U.S. history, as well as serving as a delegate to the newly formed United Nations after World War II and chairperson of its Human Rights Commission. As illustrated from this passage in her 1960 book *You Learn by Living,* Eleanor Roosevelt espoused a gregarious view to young people:

If you approach each new person you meet in a spirit of adventure, you will find that you become increasingly interested in them and endlessly fascinated by the new channels of thought and experience and personality that you encounter. I do not mean simply the famous people of the world, but people from every walk and condition of life. You will find them a source of inexhaustible surprise because of the unexpected qualities and interests which you will unearth in your search for treasure. But the treasure is there if you will mine for it.

If such a search is to be successful, however, you will need two qualities which you can develop by practice. One is the ability to be a good listener. The other is the imaginative ability to put yourself in the other's place; to try to discover what he is thinking and feeling; to understand as far as you can the background from which he came, the soil out of which his roots have grown, the customs and ideas which have shaped his thinking. You can establish an understanding relationship with people who are entirely outside your own orbit if you care enough to make the effort, to see the people you are looking at, to understand them.

Go Beyond Stereotypes

HILLARY RODHAM CLINTON

The former first lady was dogged with controversy throughout Bill Clinton's tumultuous administration. In seeking to shape public policy on such issues as national health care, she often appeared argumentative and combative. But in her new position as U.S. senator from New York, Hillary Rodham Clinton has surprised even her most audible critics with a seemingly newfound genial and nonpartisan problem-solving style. Virtually all observers of the American political scene expect her higher ambitions to manifest decisively ahead.

The world around us is changing. We see that every day. Now in the midst of such changes, it is always tempting to look for and seize upon easy answers, to use stereotypes and generalizations to describe the world, to box it up to try to make sense of it. That is, I believe, to be expected. We find ourselves sifting and sorting out all of these competing tensions and values—and sometimes if we are not careful, simplifying them to the point that we do ourselves and the times in which we live an injustice. This is one of the reasons why education, creating that tension inside where we are able to carry so many different values together to make sense of disparate pieces of information, is so critical. But we have to do it with an understanding of the importance of those with educations to stand up against the easy answers, the stereotypes, the labels.

For example, you know the kind of thing I'm talking about. We see it every day in the media: if you're under twenty-five, you're an apathetic Generation X'er. If you're over forty, you're a self-indulgent Baby Boomer. If you're a liberal, you're a bleeding heart. If you're a conservative, you have no heart. . . . The truth is that there is no single label or definition that applies to any one of us, nor to any issue that we face. Our world is too complex for that.

So we need, as difficult as it may be, to shift our thinking away from stereotypes and labels that prevent us from seeing what is happening in front of us and from having some sense of vision about what we need as a people to move forward.

Honor Your Heritage

COLIN POWELL

Raised in the Bronx by immigrant parents from Jamaica, Colin Powell rose steadily through the ranks and became America's most prominent military figure during the Gulf War. He has subsequently served as secretary of state under President George W. Bush. Though advocating an internationalist perspective, Powell has also addressed the importance of knowing one's roots.

I want you to be proud of your heritage. Study your origins. Teach your children racial pride and draw strength and inspiration from the cultures of our forebears. Not as a way of drawing back from American society and its European roots, but as a way of showing that there are other roots as well. African and Caribbean roots that are also a source of nourishment for the American family tree.

To show that African Americans are more than a product of our slave experience. To show that our varied backgrounds are as rich as that of any other American—not better or greater, but every bit as equal. Our black heritage must be a foundation stone we can build on, not a place to withdraw into.

I want you to fight racism. But remember, as Dr. King and Dr. Mandela have taught us, racism is a disease of the racist. Never let it become yours.

Keep Audacious Hope

CORNEL WEST

Professor of African American Studies at Princeton University, Cornel West is a compelling orator and noted commentator on racial affairs in the United States. His best-selling book, *Race Matters,* triggered a national debate on racial issues. West's other books include *Jews and Blacks: Let the Healing Begin,* coauthored with Michael Lerner.

There is a need for audacious hope. And it's not optimism. I'm in no way an optimist. I've been black in America for thirty-nine years. No ground for optimism here, given the progress and regress and three steps forward and four steps backward. Optimism is a notion that there's sufficient evidence that would allow us to infer that if we keep doing what we're doing, things will get better. I don't believe that.

I'm a prisoner of hope, that's something else. Cutting against the grain, against the evidence. William James said it so well in that grand and masterful 1879 essay of his called "The Sentiment of Rationality," in which he talked about faith being the courage to act when doubt is warranted. And that's what I'm talking about.

Of course, I come from a tradition, a black church tradition, in which we defined faith as stepping out on nothing and landing on something. That's the history of black folk in this country. Hope against hope. And yet still trying to sustain the notion that we world-weary and tired peoples, all peoples in this society, can be energized around causes and principles and ideals that are bigger than us, that can appeal to the better angels of our nature, so that we, in fact, can reach the conclusion that the world is incomplete, that history is unfinished, that the future is open-ended, that what we think and what we do does make a difference.

Keep On Learning

THE DALAI LAMA

Tenzin Gyatso, the fourteenth Dalai Lama (which literally means "ocean of wisdom") assumed full political power at the age of sixteen as head of state and government in 1950 when Tibet was threatened by China's might. In 1954, he met with Mao Zedong and other Chinese leaders including Chou En-lai and Deng Xiaping. In 1959, he was forced into exile in India after the Chinese military occupation of Tibet. Since 1960, he has resided in Dharamsala, aptly known as "Little Lhasa," the seat of the Tibetan government-in-exile. Since his first visit to the West in the 1970s, the Dalai Lama has met with scholars, clergy, and heads of state, and was awarded the Nobel Peace Prize in 1989. His books, highly popular in the United States and other Western countries, include *An Open Heart, Freedom in Exile, My Land and My People,* and *A Lifetime of Wisdom.*

One of the unique things about humanity is the special human brain. We have the capacity to think and to memorize. We have something that can have very, very special qualities.

Because of that, education becomes very important. I believe that education is like an instrument. Whether that instrument—that device— is used properly or constructively depends on the user. We have education, on the one hand; on the other hand, we have a good person. A good person means someone with a good heart, a sense of commitment, a sense of responsibility. Education and the warm heart, the compassionate heart; if you combine these two, then your education, your knowledge, will be constructive. Then you are yourself becoming a happy person. That is one of my fundamental beliefs: that a good heart, a warm heart, a compassionate heart, is still teachable. Please combine these two.

There is another thing I want to tell you. You have achieved your goal today, and now you are ready to begin another chapter. Now you really start real life. Real life may be more complicated. You are bound to face some unhappy things and hindrances, obstacles and complications.

So it is important to have determination and optimism and patience. If you lack patience, even when you face a small obstacle, you will lose courage. There is a Tibetan saying: "Even if you have failed at something nine times, you have still given it effort nine times." I think that's important.

HENRY KISSINGER

Henry Kissinger served as U.S. secretary of state from 1973 to 1977 in the Nixon-Ford administrations. He also held the position of assistant to the president for national security affairs, which he first assumed in 1969, until 1975. After leaving governmental service, he founded Kissinger Associates, an international consulting firm, of which he is chairman. Born in Germany to Jewish parents who fled Hitler's growing power and immigrated to New York City on the eve of World War II, Kissinger has published many books on foreign policy and global strategy issues, including *Diplomacy, Does America Need a Foreign Policy? A World Restored,* and *Years of Renewal.*

My generation grew up reading books. If you look at the history of knowledge, you can see that in the early and medieval periods, knowledge was primarily transmitted through memory. There was attendant emphasis on religion and epic poetry because those subjects everyone could agree on. The discovery of printing broadened human perspectives and introduced a secular world and a nationalist world.

Now we find that learning from books is time-consuming, and one cannot acquire all the available knowledge by reading all the books. The computer has expanded our range of knowledge in such an amazing way that we have more facts available than any previous generation. On the other hand, we acquire these facts so easily that we now know more facts than we do their meaning.

When you read a book, you somehow have to imprint in your mind the knowledge contained in it, because it's difficult to keep going back to it. When you learn from a computer, you just scan it. That you know you can always evoke the same facts again has the paradoxical consequence that we have expanded our knowledge while shrinking our perspective.

BOB TEAGUE

Bob Teague was the first African American journalist to be hired by the NBC television network. In addition to newscasting, he has been a reporter for the *Milwaukee Journal* and the *New York Times,* and written several books including *The Flip Side of Soul: Letters to My Son,* from which this selection is drawn.

Somehow I must tell you the excitement of learning. I am thinking now about my freshman course in Zoology One at Wisconsin more than thirty-five years ago. It astonished me to see certain animals, untrained by man, using tools.

A predatory fish, hovering just below the surface of a river, spits water against the underside of leaves that overhang the water, the idea being to dislodge insects squatting topside. Once the little buggers hit the surface—gulp!

An African chimp pokes a skinny stick into an underground colony of living hors d'oeuvres; when he retracts the stick, it is crawling with delicious captives. Gulp!

A huge bird lays an egg so tough she has to pick up a marble-sized rock with her beak and fling it at the egg, again and again, to break the shell and hatch her little darling.

Think for a moment, speculate. What different bright ideas might have eventually come to me and my classmates after becoming aware of such phenomena? Isn't it amazing what college professors—the Svengalis of civilization—can do with the magic of ideas? They fill young brains with the stuff that creates more room for thinking.

BARBARA WALTERS

Barbara Walters is among America's most admired TV reporters and anchors for her ability to humanize the news including complex geopolitical events. The Boston-raised Walters began her career on NBC's *Today* show, moving up the ladder from writer and researcher, to an onscreen Today Girl, to the morning show's first female host. Walters became the first woman to anchor the nightly network news when she signed with ABC in 1976, but left three years later to become a correspondent for *20/20* and eventually its coanchor. Her other TV work includes *The Barbara Walters Show,* for which she won one of her numerous Emmys, and *The View*.

This is the advice I most want to leave you with: Not everyone can be a movie star, not everyone can be a leader. These days, it seems that few want to, especially in politics. But we can learn from the leaders and from the independents, and this, finally is what I have learned.

First and foremost, you must find something you love to do. You may not know it now, but you will find it. Follow your compass, follow your gut. You must think for yourself. You are young, but you must realize how precious life is. Laugh and enjoy, and cheer yourself on in the times of adversity. You must never stop learning.

Keep Your Integrity

HARRY TRUMAN

Harry Truman's presidency was marked by such momentous events as the dropping of the atomic bomb on Japan, the Allied victory in World War II, the start of the Cold War, and the Korean War. During the decades since Truman's administration ended in 1953, historians have come to regard him with increasing respect. As a father, Truman was extremely close to his only child, Margaret, born in 1924. His many letters of advice included the following sentiments:

You are now a young lady of eighteen years young and you are responsible from now on for what Margie does. Your very excellent and efficient mother has done her duty for eighteen years. Your dad has looked on and has been satisfied with the result.

You have a good mind, a beautiful physique and a possible successful future outlook—but that now is up to you. You are the mistress of your future. All your mother and dad can do is to look on, advise when asked, and hope and wish you a happy one. There'll be troubles and sorrow a plenty, but there'll also be happy days and hard work.

Knowing Your Life's Dream

BLAIR UNDERWOOD

Blair Underwood has been a leading African American actor for nearly twenty years. Raised in Tacoma, Washington, he gained first visibility by appearances on the Bill Cosby show in the mid-1980s. His recent films include *Full Frontal, Deep Impact, The Wishing Tree,* and *G.* Underwood's prolific television roles have encompassed *Soul of the Game, City of Angels,* and *Inside TV Land: African Americans in Television.*

Firstly, you have to define your dream. What makes you tick? What makes you happy? What is the field and/or arena that you need/must explore to have satisfaction in your soul? If you can't answer that question, you will be in perpetual pursuit of nothingness, on a road nowhere and you will die . . . you die on the inside.

[The poet Langston Hughes] once wrote: "A dream deferred is like a raisin in the sun." If a dream postponed or procrastinated upon is analogous to that which is shriveled and dying, you can only imagine what life is like without any dream to speak whatsoever!

What is your dream? What are your dreams? If you don't know, find out!

Knowing Your Goals

JON BON JOVI (JOHN BONGIOVI)

Raised in New Jersey, John Bongiovi organized the band Bon Jovi in 1983 at the age of twenty-one. During the 1980s, his band won a large following and awards that included a 1987 American Music Award for Best Pop/Rock Band and a 1990 Golden Globe Award for Best Song, "Blaze of Glory," from the *Young Guns II* soundtrack. Having studied acting, Jon Bon Jovi still actively performs and records.

Some of you may have your futures mapped out. Whether it's continuing your education, conquering Wall Street, starting a *Fortune* 500 company, getting into politics, maybe becoming an entertainer.

Then there are some of you who may not have a plan yet. That's okay. Don't be embarrassed by indecision. Remember, this life is a marathon. Whatever road life leads you down, you can change direction at any time.

When I was in my early twenties, I didn't know what tomorrow would bring. Now, staring at forty, I still don't know. And that's what makes life exciting. So map out your future, but do it in pencil.

Learning to Make Choices

JOHN MCCAIN

Senator John McCain has represented Arizona since 1985 in the U.S. Senate and for two terms in the House before that. An outspoken advocate for governmental reform, especially campaign financing, he unsuccessfully challenged George W. Bush for the Republican presidential slot in 2000, but gained national visibility as a result. Admired as a Vietnam War hero, McCain has authored the best-seller *Faith of My Fathers* and, most recently, *Worth the Fighting For: What I've Learned From Mavericks, Heroes, and Politics*.

No one expects you to know at your age precisely how you will lead accomplished lives or use your talents in a cause greater than self-interest. You probably have some time before such choices and challenges confront you. Indeed, it has been my experience that such choices reveal themselves over time to every human being.

They are not choices that arrive just once and resolved at one time, thus permanently fixing the course of your life. Many of the most important choices one must make emerge slowly, sometimes obscurely through life. Often, they are choices that you must make again and again.

Once in a great while, a person is confronted with a choice or dilemma, the implications of which are so profound that its resolution may affect your life forever. But that happens only rarely, and to relatively few people. For most people, life is long enough and varied enough to account for occasional mistakes and failures.

F. Scott Fitzgerald is often recalled for his observation that, "There are no second acts in America." It's a pity that such a gifted writer is frequently remembered for this one observation, which, in my opinion, couldn't have been more mistaken. There are a great many second, third, and fourth acts for Americans in all walks of life. . . .

Bad people can occasionally do good things. Good people can occasionally do bad things. But such acts will be anomalies in a life that is defined by opposing acts. Without good character, there is no possibility that an individual will reach the end of his or her life satisfied with the experience of living. No one of good character leaves behind a wasted life, whether they die in obscurity or renown.

Learning to Take Risks

KATHRYN THORNTON

A former NASA astronaut who completed four space flights and served aboard the space shuttle *Columbia,* Kathryn Thornton grew up in Alabama and earned her doctorate in physics from the University of Virginia in 1979. Awarded a NATO Post-Doctoral Fellowship to continue her research in Heidelberg, West Germany, Thornton was selected a few years later to become an astronaut at the age of thirty-two. After a dozen years with NASA, she joined the physics faculty of the University of Virginia.

I find I am tremendously excited for the new graduates and, at the same time, somewhat apprehensive. I am excited because I know the wealth of opportunities that will be available to you; apprehensive because I know to take advantages of these opportunities will require innovativeness, perseverance when things get tough, adaptability when things don't go quite as you had expected, and above all, courage to take risks, to stick your neck out, to jump in with both feet, to go for it: all the clichés that mean to pass up a safer course of action in favor of one less certain, but one that promises great rewards. It is your willingness to risk that will in the final analysis be the yardstick by which your success will be measured.

The cost of taking risks can be very high, but the cost of not taking risks can be even higher. Five hundred years ago, Christopher Columbus sailed west from Spain in search of gold and spices in the Orient. Instead he found corn and tobacco and a new continent. He failed to reach the Orient, returned to Spain with only two of his three ships, but nevertheless, changed the face of this planet forever. . . .

Risk is what life is all about! We press the envelope, try new things that have never been done before for the sake of learning. Sometimes we fail. We need to understand those failures and accept them as a natural part of learning, of growing and taking risks.

In my office, I have a lapel button sent to me by a friend. On that button is a slogan that I think of from time to time when I am feeling a little too comfortable. It says, "The meek will inherit the earth. The rest of us will go to the stars." Each of you sitting here this morning can, if you choose, go to the stars.

Living as a True Woman

Ursula LeGuin

Ursula LeGuin is perhaps America's leading woman science-fiction and fantasy writer. The daughter of the anthropologist Alfred Kroeber, she has written more than a dozen books of imaginative fiction, including *The Dispossessed, The Left Hand of Darkness, Malafrena,* and *The Compass Rose.* LeGuin is also the author of a fantasy series for children, the *Earthsea* trilogy. A longtime resident of Portland, Oregon, LeGuin has won numerous awards including the *Boston Globe*–Hornbook Award for Juvenile Fiction and the National Book Award for the children's novel *The Farthest Shore.*

In our society, women have lived, and have been despised for living, the whole side of life that includes and takes responsibility for helplessness, weakness, and illness, for the irrational and the irreparable, for all that is obscure, passive, uncontrolled, animal, unclean—the valley of the shadow, the deep, the depths of life. . . .

So what I hope for you is that you live there not as prisoners, ashamed of being women, consenting captives of a psychopathic social system, but as natives. That you will be at home there, keep house there, be your own mistress, with a room of your own. That you will do your work there, whatever you're good at, art or science or tech or running a company, or sweeping under the beds, and when they tell you that it's second-class work because a woman is doing it, I hope you tell them to go to hell and that they're going to give you equal pay for equal time.

I hope you live without the need to dominate, and without the need to be dominated. I hope you are never victims, but I hope you have no power over other people. And when you fail, and are defeated, and in pain, and in the dark, then I hope you will remember that darkness is your country, where you live, where no wars are fought and no wars are won, but where the future is.

Our roots are in the dark, the earth is our country. Why did we look up for blessing, instead of around, and down? What hope we have lies there. Not in the sky full of orbiting spy-eyes and weaponry, but in the earth we have looked down upon. Not from above, but from below. Not in the light that blinds, but in the dark that nourishes, where human beings grow human souls.

Living Responsibly
in the Present

JAMES RESTON

James "Scotty" Reston was one of America's leading journalists for many decades. He joined the *New York Times* in 1940, later served as its Washington bureau chief, and won the Pulitzer Prize. Reston's first assignment for the *New York Times* was as a member of its London staff during World War II. The Nazis' fierce bombing, which he experienced in the Battle of Britain, shaped his subsequent view of the world:

It is not surprising that old men look back. They have always done so, and for many excellent reasons, they must continue to do so. But a backward approach, especially at this time, has its limitations. . . .

There have been generations in this country which enjoyed the luxury of merely carrying on the work of their fathers, more or less as it was done before, but yours is not one of them. You are going to have to experiment and pioneer again. You are going to have to reexamine, with objective open-mindedness, many things that have been taken for granted by your fathers. . . .

The time and place are different, and the instruments of tyranny are far greater than in the time of Napoleon, but the challenge to liberty is very much the same. Whether we like it or not, we are the inheritors of a great cause, and I am suggesting that we should not rail against fate, but . . . clasp it eagerly, as the will of God.

Living Your Life as a Novel

MARY HIGGINS CLARK

Mary Higgins Clark is among America's leading mystery writers, with best-selling novels including *A Cry in the Night, Moonlight Becomes You, The Lottery Winner,* and *The Cradle Will Fall.* Born and raised in New York City, she began writing magazine pieces, then scripts for radio stations, and eventually books. Among Clark's numerous awards are thirteen honorary doctorates and the Grand Prix de Literature of France, received in 1980. She has served as president of the Mystery Writers of America and chairman of the International Crime Congress.

I'm not a statesman who can offer you an overall view of the world situation, a philosopher who can reduce the secret of a successful future into a few succinct sentences. My area of expertise is in writing suspense novels, so I'm going to talk a little about writing a suspense novel because, in effect, you grads are beginning to write a suspense novel today and the title of it is *The Future.*

A novel requires certain ingredients: the setting, the plot, the protagonist, the good guys and the bad guys, the victories, the downward steps, the red herrings, the clues that may escape us, the heart-pounding tension, and finally, resolution, climax, denouement.

Your novel is opening today in the setting of this arena. The plot is what you do with the rest of your life. You are the protagonist. The opening sentence is terribly important. The joke in suspense writing is that a perfect opening sentence is, "A shot rang out in the night."

I offer you what I think is totally meaningful for you today. "The graduate knew that the moment the diploma was placed in his or her hand, nothing would ever be the same."

The people who will be important in your lives are the characters in your book. Some are already in place: family, friends, neighbors, teachers, perhaps even the love interest. Along the way, new people will walk through your chapters. Some will enliven the prose, will add color and depth and meaning. Some will show you great goodness. Others are the ones who deserve your help. Still others may impede the story, distract you from the goal.

Your novel should contain a quest. Someone or something has to be found. For most of you, the primary quest of the moment is to find the job that will bring out the best in you, the one that will fulfill you. Maybe you'll start working for it now; maybe further education is essential.

Here I, as editorial adviser, offer a suggestion. You're going to be working for a long time. There's a marvelous truism. "If you want to be happy for a year, win the lottery. If you want to be happy for life, love what you do." I firmly believe that the legendary godmothers stand around our cradles and leave each one of us at least one special gift. The one that was offered to me was storytelling. Try to find the one that was granted to you.

Look Inside Yourself

A̲N̲N̲A̲ ̲Q̲U̲I̲N̲D̲L̲E̲N̲

Today is the day that those lucky enough to be your teachers, your class-mates, your friends, and your family must say: custody of your life belongs in full to you and you alone. Do not cede it to anyone else, no matter how loving or well intentioned. People will tell you what you ought to study and how you ought to feel. They will tell you what to read and how to live. They will urge you to take jobs they themselves loathe, and to follow safe paths they themselves find tedious. Don't listen.

This is tough stuff. It's so much easier to follow the template, to walk the straight and narrow set out by the culture, the family, the friends, the focus groups. You will have to bend all your will not to march to the music that all of those great "theys" that pipe on their flutes. They want you to go to professional school, to pierce your navel, to wear khakis, to tint your hair, to bare your soul. These are the fashionable ways. The music is tinny, if you listen close enough. Look inside, look inside. This will always be your struggle.

Looking Back on Your Life

Mark Twain

Mark Twain, the pen name of Missouri-born Samuel Clemens, is one of America's most intriguing literary figures. In late-nineteenth-century novels like *The Adventures of Huckleberry Finn, The Prince and the Pauper,* and *A Connecticut Yankee in King Arthur's Court,* Twain combined homespun humor with biting social criticism. He was also a witty, entertaining, and prolific public speaker. In his last decades, Twain's lectures included college commencements.

[In visiting my hometown recently], you cannot know what a strain it was on my emotions. In fact, when I found myself shaking hands with persons I had not seen for fifty years and looking into wrinkled faces that were so young and joyous when I last saw them, I experienced emotions that I had never expected and did not know were in me. I was profoundly moved and saddened to think that this was the last time that I would ever behold those kind old faces and dear old scenes of childhood. . . .

I have seen it stated in print that as a boy I had been guilty of stealing peaches, apples, and watermelons. I read a story to this effect very closely not long ago, and I was convinced of one thing, which was that the man who wrote it was of the opinion that it was wrong to steal, and that I had not acted in the right in doing so. I wish now, however, to make an honest statement, which is that I do not believe, in all my checkered career, I stole a ton of peaches.

One night I stole—I mean I removed—a watermelon from a wagon while the owner was attending to another customer. I crawled off to a secluded spot, where I found that it was green. It was the greenest melon in the Mississippi Valley. Then I began to reflect. I began to be sorry. I wondered what George Washington would have done had he been in my place. I thought a long time, and then suddenly felt that strange feeling which comes to a man with a good resolution, and took up that watermelon and took it back to its owner. I handed him the watermelon and told him to reform. He took my lecture much to heart, and, when he gave me a good one in place of the green melon, I forgave him.

I told him that I would still be a customer of his, and that I cherished no ill-feeling because of the incident—that would remain green in my memory.

Making a Better World

Maya Angelou

When Maya Angelou read her newest poem at former President Bill Clinton's 1993 inauguration, it was another landmark achievement in her multifaceted career. The author of numerous magazine articles and more than ten books, including *I Know Why the Caged Bird Sings, I Shall Not Be Moved,* and *Now Sheba Sings the Song,* Angelou has earned both Pulitzer Prize and National Book Award nominations.

Maya was the second child and only daughter of urban African American parents. She was sent, along with her brother, Bailey, to be raised by her paternal grandmother, a storekeeper in Stamps, Arkansas. Working with Dr. Martin Luther King, Jr. during the 1960s, Angelou has gained acclaim as an actress, playwright, and director and has made hundreds of television appearances. She also teaches American Studies at Wake Forest University in North Carolina.

You are obliged to bring down the walls of ignorance, the walls of racism and sexism and ageism, and all those walls that keep us apart, keep us limping. . . .

There's a statement of Terence that I would ask you to keep as a memento: "I am a human being. Nothing human can be alien to me."

He was an African, a slave sold to a Roman senator. Freed by that senator, he became the most popular playwright in Rome. Six of his plays and that one statement have come down to us from 154 B.C. This man, not born white or free, or with any chance of ever achieving citizenship in Rome, said, "I am a human being. Nothing human can be alien to me."

This statement liberates you. Suddenly you are able to reach into the teachings of Aristotle, James Weldon Johnson, Nikki Giovanni, Emily Dickinson. You are able to reach into the statements, into the hearts, of Paul Laurence Dunbar and García Lorca and Márquez, and all the writers, all the dreamers, all the hopers—so you do not have to be forever bound and strangled by the ignorance of someone who went before you.

Bono (Paul Hewson)

As lead singer-songwriter for the phenomenally popular Dublin rock band U2, Bono has been featured on *Time*'s cover for his energetic humanitarian efforts, particularly lobbying the U.S. government to ease the debt of Third World nations. He was originally nicknamed "Bono Vox" by a high school chum, who took it from a Dublin hearing-aid store; fittingly enough, the original moniker meant "good voice" in cockeyed Latin. Paul later shortened it to Bono, which remains his stage name to date. At times satirized in the British press for his world-saving zealousness, Bono combines his hugely successful musical career with tireless social activism.

My name is Bono, and I'm a rock star. Now, I tell you this not as a boast, but more as a kind of confession. Because in my view the only thing worse than a rock star is a rock star with a conscience—a celebrity with a cause—a placard-waving, knee-jerking, fellow-traveling activist with a

Lexus and a swimming pool shaped like his head. I'm a singer. When you need twenty thousand people screaming your name in order to feel good about your day, you know you're a singer.

I owe more than my spoiled lifestyle to rock music. I owe my worldview. Music was like an alarm clock for me as a teenager and still keeps me from falling asleep in the comfort of my freedom.

Rock music to me is rebel music. But rebelling against what? In the 1950s, it was sexual mores and double standards. In the 1960s, it was the Vietnam War and racial and social inequality. What are we rebelling against now? If I am honest, I'm rebelling against my own indifference. I am rebelling against the idea that the world is the way the world is, and there's not a damned thing I can do about it. So I'm trying to do a damned thing. But fighting my indifference is my own problem. What's your problem? . . .

Isn't "Love thy neighbor" in the global village so inconvenient? God writes us these lines but we have to sing them, take them to the top of the charts.

BEN COHEN

Cofounder with his friend Jerry Greenfield of Ben & Jerry's ice cream company based in Vermont, Ben Cohen has zealously sought to make their business a model for twenty-first-century commerce. Its mission has emphasized community, and even global responsibility, as well as maximizing employee benefit from the company's success.

Except for maximizing profits, many businesses tend to be valueless. When we as employees walk into a business at nine in the morning, the message we get is to leave our values at the door. You're here to earn a living and to maximize profits, and if you have some social concern that you want to deal with, do it at home or in your spare time and give a few dollars to whomever knocks at your door. And yet it is just when we as human beings are organized in our most powerful force as a business that we are able to deal with the social problems that confront our society, and it is just at that point that we are forbidden from doing so.

What we are discovering at Ben & Jerry's is that there is a spiritual aspect to business, just as there is to the lives of individuals. Just because the idea that the good that you do comes back to you is written in the Bible and not in some business textbook doesn't mean that it is any less valid. We are all interconnected. As we help others, we cannot help but to help ourselves.

Well, this is a pretty new consciousness for business, and it represents a real paradigm shift from a win/lose scenario, where it's business versus consumers, business versus the environment, business versus society, to a win/win scenario, where it's business working to help its consumers, business working to help society and the environment. It's a shift back to biblical values, but as a paradigm shift it meets with incredible resistance. Here's what the German philosopher Arthur Schopenhauer had to say about situations like this: All truth passes through three stages. First, it is ridiculed. Second, it is violently opposed. Third, it is accepted as being self-evident.

Coretta Scott King

As the widow of Martin Luther King, Jr., Coretta Scott King has long been active in the fight for civil and human rights, and became an international icon for her efforts to promote nonviolent social change. Raised in rural Alabama before World War II, she won a scholarship in 1945 to Ohio's Antioch College to study music and elementary education, and in 1948 debuted as a vocalist at the Second Baptist Church. Later, while studying classical singing at the Boston Conservatory of Music, she met and married Martin Luther King, Jr., then a doctoral student at Boston University. After his assassination in 1968, Coretta Scott King continued to lead major demonstrations in support of striking workers and the poor, and in 1969, as a tribute to his memory, founded the Atlanta-based Center for Nonviolent Social Change. Serving as its president and chief executive officer, she has maintained a high public profile in the United States and abroad.

When you are in an academic environment and, later in life, if you work in an environment where most of the people are well educated, there is a tendency to take a good education for granted. But I want everyone here to meditate for a moment on an interesting statistic I recently came across, which will help you put into perspective what a college education means. And that fact is that only one percent of the people on earth have a college degree.

Think about it. Only one of every one hundred people in the world have a college degree. No matter how common well-educated people seem to be in the United States, understand that you are now members of an elite and privileged group. I say "privileged" because even if you worked hard to get to this day, you must understand that God chose you to be a part of that one percent.

Now, just because you are a member of an elite group, that doesn't mean you have a license to start acting like an elitist. On the contrary, God made it possible for you to get a good education, so you could use what you have learned, not only to have a good income and a comfortable life for yourself and your family, but also to help other people have a better life. You are here today because you have been called to serve.

TED KOPPEL

Ted Koppel has won every major broadcasting award, including thirty-seven Emmys and two Sigma Delta Chi Awards, the highest honor bestowed for public service by the Society of Professional Journalists. A native of Lancashire, England, he immigrated with his family to the United States as a child, and joined ABC News as a full-time correspondent at the age of twenty-three. Before becoming *Nightline*'s anchor and managing editor at ABC News, Koppel covered Henry Kissinger's famous "shuttle diplomacy" in the mid-1970s and coauthored the best-seller *In the National Interest* with his friend and colleague Marvin Kalb, formerly of CBS News.

What is great about our system of law and government is precisely its focus on the rights and obligations of the individual. There is in our system a touching faith in the power of one man, one woman to make a difference, and in each individual's right to challenge what are, after all, only the symbols of our greatness. Burn a flag and you've simply destroyed a piece of paper or cloth that can easily be replaced. Deny the right to burn that flag and you have destroyed something irreparable.

We will not change what's wrong with our culture through legislation, or by choosing sides on the basis of personal popularity or party affiliation. We will change it by small acts of courage and kindness, by recognizing, each of us, his or her own obligation to set a proper example.

Aspire to decency. Practice civility toward one another. Admire and emulate ethical behavior wherever you find it. Apply a rigid standard of morality to your lives, and if periodically you fail, as you surely will, adjust your lives, not the standards.

Measuring Success

JONNY MOSELEY

Olympic gold medalist Jonny Moseley was born in Puerto Rico and moved to northern California with his family as a child. He began skiing on his older brother's dare. He showed extraordinary talent as a skier, and entered his first competition within a few years. Moseley made the U.S. Ski Team in 1993 at the age of eighteen, but narrowly missed out on a spot to attend the 1994 Winter Olympic Games in Lillehammer. In 1998, Moseley won several skiing medals including a gold medal at the Winter Olympics in Nagano, Japan, and became the celebrity of his hometown of Tiburon, California.

Today the experts give you your diploma. I'm not telling you to go for fourth place, but I encourage you to be free in the way you measure your success. I don't claim to know what it will be like to be in your position, but I know that when you leave here, grades will be handed out differently. Your ability to gauge your success will largely depend on how you perceive it. How you choose to perceive it is entirely up to you. Your perception of this intangible ideal called success is something you can control. You can shape it, set it up, feel it, and define it. Allow competition to turn inward. If you do not depend on awards, money, or other validations to dictate your well-being and your measure of success, you will own your happiness.

Planning Your Career

THEODORE ROOSEVELT

Theodore Roosevelt was the youngest man ever to become U.S. president. He was forty-two when McKinley was assassinated in 1901. Roosevelt grew up frail and sickly with asthma, and suffered as a child his father's early death. With his mother's encouragement, he deliberately strengthened himself by vigorous exercise and sports. Later, as an admired Rough Rider and an influential political leader for a generation, he made the phrase "Speak softly and carry a big stick" famous and counseled his children to "Hit the line hard." Yet Roosevelt always valued character and intelligence more than physical prowess.

Writing from the White House in January 1904, President Roosevelt offered this lucid guidance to his son Theodore Jr. at Harvard:

I have great confidence in you. I believe you have the ability, and above all the energy, the perseverance and the common sense, to win out in civil life. That you will have some hard times and some discouraging times I have no question; but this is merely another way of saying that you will share the common lot. Though you have to work in different ways from those in which I worked, you will not have to work any harder, nor to face periods of more discouragement. I trust in your ability, and especially your character, and I am confident you will win.

In the Army and the Navy, the chance for a man to show great ability and rise above his fellows does not occur on the average more than once in a generation. When I was down in Santiago, it was melancholy for me to see how fossilized and lacking in ambition, and generally useless, were most of the men of my age and over who had served their lives in the Army. . . . I want you to think over all these matters very seriously. It would be a great misfortune for you start in the Army or Navy as a career, and find that you had mistaken your desires and had gone in without really weighing the matter.

Putting Your Values to Work

JACK KEMP

An eighteen-year congressman from the Buffalo area and secretary of housing and urban development in the Bush administration, Kemp made an unsuccessful bid for the vice presidency in 1996 running alongside presidential candidate Bob Dole. Emphasizing the importance of bringing new business and capital to revitalize impoverished urban areas, Kemp created and heads Empower America. Before entering politics, he was a professional football player for thirteen years, serving on the San Diego Chargers and the Buffalo Bills.

This is the time when we need men and women of courage and conviction who will stand up. We're not the captain of the Dodgers, but we're the captain of our own souls. And the soul of America is in how we treat the less fortunate. The soul of America is in what we do about the Third World. The soul of America is in what we do in our neighborhoods that are hurting and in despair and in lack of opportunity.

We are the ones who must stand up and hold our arms around all men and women of goodwill who want a chance to be what God meant them to be, not what the state wants them to be.

Raising Children Well

GEORGE BUSH SR.

The forty-first U.S. president is undoubtedly best known today for his leadership during the Gulf War. Persuasively assembling a broad international coalition to roll back Iraq from its invasion of Kuwait, he was unable, however, to sustain a broad domestic agenda or translate his foreign policy success into greater political currency for his administration. Still, having raised sons to become a U.S. president and a governor of Florida, George Bush would seem to be the perfect candidate to offer insights about fatherly effectiveness.

Parents must read to their children and instill a love of learning. Government can, and we must, fight crime. But fathers and mothers must teach discipline and instill those values in their children. Government can, and we must, foster American competitiveness. But parents must teach their children the dignity of work and instill a work ethic in the kids. And to paraphrase that fantastic philosopher, Barbara Bush, what you teach at your house is more important than what happens at the White House. And she is absolutely correct on that.

All us realize that merely knowing what's right is not enough. We must then do what's right. Today I'm asking you to carefully consider the personal decisions that you'll make about marriage and how you will raise your children. Ultimately, your decisions about right and wrong, about loyalty and integrity, and yes, even self-sacrifice, will determine the quality of all the other decisions you'll make.

Reading Poetry for Inspiration

ROBERTSON DAVIES

Raised in rural Canada after World War I, Davies was an editor, playwright, and novelist. After spending a few years in theatrical life and journalism, he conducted most of his professional career at the University of Toronto. His many books include *The Cunning Man, Reading and Writing, The Rebel Angels,* and *The Lyre of Orpheus.*

Get yourself a good anthology of poetry and keep it by your bedside. Read a little before you go to sleep. Read a little if you wake up in the middle of the night. When you are idle during the day—on public transport, or at a committee meeting—let your mind dwell on what you have read. One book will last you a long time. Indeed it may last you a lifetime.

Remembering to Have Fun

Pat Metheny

Guitarist Pat Metheny is that rarity, a jazz musician who has obtained an impressive popular success, and at the same time remains an innovative player with a personal voice. Born in suburban Kansas City in 1954, he began playing guitar at the age of thirteen. He gained his first recording with pianist Paul Bley, but it was with vibist Gary Burton's group that Metheny initially became well known. Forming his own band, The Pat Metheny Group, in 1978, he recorded numerous albums on the ECM label both alone and with his quartet, in addition to working with musicians such as Ornette Coleman, Bruce Hornsby, Joshua Redman, and Joni Mitchell.

All of you here have roads ahead of you that will be filled with good musical days, the ones where you feel you can play or hear anything, and bad musical days [too]. But that variety, that sense of unknowing, that feeling of having to make it up yourself, that sense of adventure, that is what music is. And that is a big part of why having a life as a musician is so much fun.

And "fun" is a good word to end on. Because the last thing, and maybe the most important thing, that I've noticed over the years of playing with people from all kinds of stylistic zones and all different kinds of music—from Sonny Rollins to Steve Reich, from David Bowie to Milton Nascimiento, from Herbie Hancock to Gary Burton—is just how much fun they all have doing what they do, when they are doing it at their best.

For all the satisfaction and work and practice and dues that it takes to become a good musician, in the end, it's a blast to be a musician . . . Play [well] and have fun.

Reminiscing About College

JERRY SEINFELD

Jerry Seinfeld's brand of "observational humor" has made him one of America's most popular and imitated comedians. Born in Brooklyn, raised in suburban Massapequa ("It's an old Indian name that means 'by the mall'"), Seinfeld began the comedy club circuit the night after he graduated from Queens College. He performed stand-up for free at times just to perfect his act. Seinfeld's big break came when he became a regular guest on *Late Night With David Letterman* and the *Tonight* show. Network and cable specials followed, and in 1990 he was given the creative outlet of a lifetime: his own network sitcom. After nine successful seasons, Seinfeld decided to end the program, which won a 1993 Emmy for best comedy series, and pursue other creative activities, including marriage and child-rearing.

I spent several wonderful years here. The best spot I ever got was in my junior year. It was right out here on Kissena Boulevard and Melbourne Avenue. I didn't even have to parallel [park]. I pulled right in. It was such a beautiful spot.

My only regret is if I could have foreseen that I would be standing here today, when my parents were pushing me to become a doctor, I could have at least said to them, "All right, all right, just let me tell jokes to strangers in nightclubs for eighteen years, and I'm sure after that they'll make me a doctor.

Several years later in a *New York Times* interview, Seinfeld reminisced about his career accomplishments. With sentiments eminently applicable to young graduates, he commented: "You have to motivate yourself with challenges. That's how you know you're still alive. Once you start doing only what you've proven you can do, you're on the road to death."

Rise Above Commercialism

Henry David Thoreau

Henry David Thoreau was an American writer who, in works such as *Walden, The Maine Woods,* and *A Week on the Concord and Merrimack Rivers,* has become an icon for his celebration of nature and simple living, and his opposition to anti-human institutions of his era, especially slavery. Born and raised in Concord, Massachussetts, Thoreau became close with the older, far more successful writer-philosopher Ralph Waldo Emerson, whose transcendentalist spiritual outlook he heartily shared. Spurned in his midthirties by the one woman whom he loved, Thoreau remained a lonely bachelor, crafting beautiful essays—about nature and the human soul—prolifically, which gave him a devoted following but brought meager financial reward.

The characteristic of our epoch is perfect freedom—freedom of thought and action. The indignant Greek, the oppressed Pole, the jealous American assert it. The skeptic no less than the believer, the heretic no less than the faithful child of the Church, have begun to enjoy it. It has generated an unusual degree of energy and activity; it has generated the *commercial spirit.* Man thinks faster and freer than ever before. He, moreover, moves faster and freer. He is more restless, because he is more independent than ever. The winds and the waves are not enough for him; he must need ransack the bowels of the earth, that he may make for himself a highway of iron over its surface.

[But] let men, true to their natures, cultivate the moral affections, lead manly and independent lives; let them make riches the means and not the ends of existence, and we shall hear no more of the commercial spirit.

The sea will not stagnate, the earth will be as green as ever, and the air as pure. This curious world which we inhabit is more wonderful than it is useful; it is more to be admired and enjoyed than used. . . . The human race is making one more advance in that infinite series of progressions which waits it.

We glory in those very excesses which are a source of anxiety to the wise and good; as an evidence that man will not always be the slave of matter, but ere long, casting off those earth-born desires which identify him with the brute, shall the days of his sojourn in this, his nether Paradise.

Rise Above Your Teachers

ALBERT EINSTEIN

Albert Einstein, the Nobel Prize–winning genius who transformed human understanding of space and time, was typically patient with those who sought his approval or endorsement for their own intellectual or scientific efforts. Having been viewed as mentally deficient as a child at a regimented German school, Einstein was especially sympathetic to those interested in educational reform and progressive methods. In his 1937 book, *The World as I See It*, Einstein presented his friendly advice given to a letter writer who sent her book-in-progress:

I have read about sixteen pages of your manuscript and it made me smile. It is clever, well observed, honest, [and] it stands on its own two feet up to a point. I suffered exactly the same treatment at the hands of my teachers, who disliked me most for my independence and passed me over when they wanted assistants (I must admit that I was somewhat less of a model student than you).

But it would not have been worth my while to write anything about my school life, still less would I have liked to be responsible for anyone's printing or actually reading it. Besides, one always cuts a poor figure if one complains about others who are still struggling for their place in the sun too after their own fashion.

Therefore pocket your temperament and keep your manuscript for your sons and daughters, in order they may derive consolation from it and—not give a damn for what their teachers tell them or think of them. . . .

The only rational way of educating is to be an example—of what to avoid, if one can't be the other sort.

Rules for Living Well

ALAN ALDA

Alan Alda is undoubtedly best known for his role of Hawkeye on the long-running TV series *M*A*S*H*. Raised in New York City, Alda studied at Fordham University. In the late 1970s and '80s, his genial personality made him everyone's ideal of the "sensitive man." Alda has won Emmys for both acting and directing. His popular movies include *What Women Want, Mad City, Flirting With Disaster, The Object of My Affection,* and *Murder at 1600*.

I want you to focus that hope [you feel today] and level that excitement into coherent rays that will strike like a laser at the targets of our discontent. I want you to be potent; to do good when you can and to hold your wit and your intelligence like a shield against other people's wantonness. And above all, to laugh and enjoy yourself in a life of your own choosing and in a world of your own making.

I want you to be strong and aggressive and tough and resilient and full of feeling. I want you to have *chutzpah*. Columbus had *chutzpah*. The signers of the Declaration of Independence had *chutzpah*. Don't ever aim your doubt at yourself. Laugh at yourself, but don't doubt yourself. . . .

Be bold. Let the strength of your desire give force and moment to your every step. Move with all of yourself. When you embark for strange places, don't leave any of yourself safely on shore.

Have the nerve to live life creatively. The creative is the place where no one else has ever been. It is not the previously known. You have to leave the city of your comfort and go into the wilderness of your intuition. You can't get there by bus, only by hard work and risk and by not quite knowing what you're doing, but what you'll discover will be wonderful. What you'll discover will be yourself.

RUSSELL BAKER

Russell Baker, a double Pulitzer Prize–winning journalist, is best known for his political satire. Starting as a reporter for his hometown newspaper, the *Baltimore Sun,* Baker joined the *New York Times* in 1954. Eight years later, he launched his "Observer" column, with its far-reaching—and widely syndicated—humorous observations about American life and politics. Baker's many books include the bestselling memoir *Growing Up, Looking Back,* and *The Good Times.*

Over the years, I spoke to many graduating classes, always pleading with them: Whatever you do, do not go forth. Nobody listened. They kept right on going forth anyhow. . . . So I will not waste my breath today pleading with you not to go forth. Instead I will limit myself to a single plea. When you get out there in the world, try not to make it any worse than it already is. I thought it might help to give you a list of . . . ten things:

One: Bend down once in a while to smell a flower.

Two: Don't go around in clothes that talk. There is already too much talk in the world. We've got so many talking people there's hardly anybody left to listen . . . If you simply cannot resist being an incompetent klutz, don't boast about it by wearing a T-shirt that says, "Underachiever and proud of it." Being dumb is not the worst thing in the world, but letting your clothes shout it loud depresses the neighbors and embarrasses your parents.

Three: Listen once in a while. It's amazing what you can hear.

Four: Sleep in the nude. In an age when people don't even get dressed to go to the theater anymore, it's silly getting dressed up to go to bed.

Five: Turn off your TV once or twice a month and pick up a book. It will ease your blood pressure. It might even wake up your mind, but if it puts you to sleep, you're still a winner.

Six: Don't take your gun to town. Don't even leave it home unless you lock all your bullets in a safe deposit box in a faraway bank.

Seven: Learn to fear automobiles. It is not the trillion-dollar deficit that will finally destroy America. It is the automobile.

Eight: Have some children. Children add texture to your life. They will save you from turning into old fogies before you're middle-aged. They will teach you humility.

Nine: Get married. I know you don't want to hear this, but getting married will give you a lot more satisfaction in the long run than your BMW ... What's more, without marriage you will have practically no material at all to work with when you decide to write a book or hire a psychiatrist.

Ten: Smile. You're one of the luckiest people in the world. You're living in America. Enjoy it.

BARBARA BUSH

Barbara Bush is unique in recent American history as both a former first lady and mother of a sitting U.S. president. Though her husband's forty-first presidential administration was embroiled in bipartisan controversy, Barbara Bush constantly maintained an image of what she jokingly called "everybody's grandmother." Her white hair, relaxed manner, and keen wit have indeed been disarming traits. Her *Millie's Book* presented anecdotes about the Bush family dog, and was followed by the best-selling *Barbara Bush: A Memoir,* published in 1994. She currently heads the Barbara Bush Foundation for Family Literacy.

I hope that many of you will consider making three very special choices.

The first is to believe in something larger than yourself, to get involved in some of the big ideas of our time. I chose literacy because I honestly believe that if more people could read, write, and comprehend, we could be that much closer to solving so many of the problems that plague our nation and our society.

Early on, I made another choice which I hope you will make as well. Whether you are talking about education, career, or service, you are talking about life, and life really must have joy. It's supposed to be fun!

One of the reasons I made the most important decision of my life— to marry George Bush—is because he made me laugh. It's true, sometimes we've laughed through our tears, but that shared laughter has been one of our strongest bonds. Find the joy in life. . . .

The third choice that must not be missed is to cherish your human connections: your relationship with family and friends. For several years, you've had impressed upon you the importance to your career of dedication and hard work, and of course, that's true. But as important as your obligations as a doctor, lawyer, or business leader will be, you are a human being first, and those human connections—with spouses, with children, with friends—are the most important investments you will ever make.

At the end of your life, you will never regret not having passed one more test, not winning one more verdict, or not closing one more deal. You will regret time not spent with a husband, a child, a friend, or a parent.

DORIS KEARNS GOODWIN

Doris Kearns Goodwin is acclaimed as one of America's leading historians and political biographers. She served as President Lyndon Johnson's assistant in producing his memoirs, and later married Richard Goodwin, writer and adviser to John and Robert Kennedy. Such contacts led to her popular books, *Lyndon Johnson and the American Dream* and *Fitzgeralds and the Kennedys: An American Saga*. In 1995, Doris Kearns Goodwin was awarded the Pulitzer Prize for her biography of Franklin and Eleanor Roosevelt, *No Ordinary Time*. She then turned to writing a memoir of her own, about growing up as a Brooklyn Dodgers fan, *Wait Till Next Year*. Doris Kearns Goodwin is a regular political commentator for TV and radio.

As you figure out the kind of work you want to do, the challenge is to find work imbued with meaning, work that provides enjoyment on a daily basis. If you choose a career for money or prestige or security but dislike going to work more than not, it will never be worth it in the long run. As for the sphere of play, I've learned over the years that even with sports and recreation and hobbies, there's a need for a level of commitment of time and energy deep enough to really enjoy something and be able to derive relaxation from it. . . .

As for the final sphere of love and friendship, I can only say that it gets harder once the natural communities of college and hometown are gone. It takes work and commitment, demands toleration for human frailties, forgiveness for the inevitable disappointments and betrayals that come even with the best of relationships.

GABE PRESSMAN

Gabe Pressman is extolled in New York City's broadcast journalism community as the "reporter's reporter." Raised in the Bronx, he has been associated with NBC News for more than thirty-five years, and is credited with inventing the craft of street journalism. During his long tenure at WNBC Channel 4 News, Pressman has achieved a peerless record of investigative reporting on politics and social issues including homelessness. He has won eight Emmys and many other awards.

I was fortunate to get into television news early. I had the advantage of being on the scene at the beginning. It's impossible to predict what the challenges will be for you. I would suggest that you keep your options open—that you not fear to get into new fields and accept new challenges. Life is trial and error. The important thing is to stay in there and keep punching.

What a glorious time this can be for you and yours. It's no accident that it's called a commencement, a beginning. A new beginning for all of you, and, if there's any wisdom I can impart, it is that you should be true to yourself and not to fear to undertake any challenge. As Shakespeare said—and as a journalist I can't resist calling on expert opinions—as Shakespeare said, "This above all, to thine own self be true and it must follow, as the night the day, thou cans't not then be false to any man."

The immortal bard wasn't politically correct. I would make that "thou cans't not then be false to any person."

GEORGE PLIMPTON

George Plimpton has uniquely produced a career spanning journalism, book writing, editing, and acting. His well-known participatory interests include professional sports and celebrity culture. "There are people who would perhaps call me a dilettante," he once quipped, "because it looks as though I'm having too much fun. I have never been convinced there's anything inherently wrong in having fun." Plimpton's many books include *Truman Capote, Pet Peeves, Open Net,* and *Playwrights at Work.*

I once contributed to a collection of graduation speeches published in a book, and the other day, I went through the speeches to dig out what my fellow speakers had come up with in the name of advice. Here is a sampling:

> Never lose faith.
> Love one another.
> Raise strong families.
> Find out about your grandmother's grandfather.
> Walk across the Brooklyn Bridge.
> Lay off the television.
> Make a chocolate cake.
> Fill a pothole with hot asphalt.
> Listen to your own drumming.
> Don't just sit there and look at a bell. Ring it.
> Smell a flower.

Sleep in the nude.
Don't play it safe.
Equip yourself with a baloney detection kit.
Believe in yourself.
Believe in America.
Turn up the heat.
Indulge the cool in you.
Find every ounce of the messy plutonium.
Lean against the wind.
Always keep the shower curtain inside the bathtub.
Unpack, go back to your [college] rooms.

MARIA SHRIVER

A contributing anchor for *Dateline NBC* and contributing correspondent for MSNBC, Maria Shriver has been active in the broadcasting news field for more than fifteen years. Her recent best-sellers have included the children's book *What's Heaven?* and *Ten Things I Wish I'd Known Before I Went Out Into the Real World,* an expansion of the advice conveyed in this commencement speech:

[My] top ten list of things I wish someone had told me when I was sitting, like you, at my graduation:

Pinpoint your passion.
No job is beneath you.

Who you work for and with is as important as what you do.

Your behavior has consequences.

Be willing to fail.

Superwoman is dead.

Children do not change your career.

Marriage is hard work.

Don't expect anyone else to support you financially.

Laughter and a sense of humor about yourself will smooth the road before you.

Rules for Success

SEAN CONNERY

Sean Connery is among the world's leading actors. Linked closely with the glamorous James Bond role he played for several years, Connery grew up in a working-class Scottish family during the Depression and held many jobs, including laborer and lifeguard before his acting career was successfully launched at MGM in the late 1950s. Recipient of numerous professional awards, he was knighted by the British government in 2000. Connery's recent films include *Dragonheart, Finding Forrester, Entrapment, The Rock,* and *The Avengers.* In *Sean Connery: From 007 to Hollywood Icon,* biographer Andrew Yule recounted the actor's career advice to his teenage son.

Until he was sixteen, Jason had wanted to be a veterinarian. It was hanging around listening to the conversations between his father and show business friends that brought about the change to acting, as well as the recognition that the hunger his father had known, to get out and make something of himself, existed in him too. Different though it was with his privileged background, the similarity lay in wanting to be the best he possibly could at whatever he took up, and to succeed on his own, rather than ride on his father's coattails.

There was one major hurdle to overcome with Jason's decision to take up acting, he was terrified what his father would think, and was completely nonplussed when a favorable reaction was evinced.

"I thought you wouldn't like it," he managed to stammer.

"Why shouldn't I?" Connery asked." "I think it's terrific." He had just two pieces of advice for his son: "If you have enthusiasm, you'll succeed," followed by "Look out for sharks!"

CALLIE KHOURI

Raised in Texas and Kentucky by her doctor parents, Khouri went to Purdue University to study landscape architecture, but switched to drama. After moving to Los Angeles to pursue a career in films, she achieved fame with her script for *Thelma and Louise*. Later scripts have included *Something to Talk About, Rock Star,* and *Divine Secrets of the Ya-Ya Sisterhood,* which she also directed.

Along the way, I learned some things I thought I'd pass along to you in the hope that maybe, at the very least, I could save you some time . . . My first big tip:

Don't worry about what people will think of you, because first of all, they're not thinking about you. In all likelihood, they're worried about what you're thinking about them. Anybody who thinks less of you for following a dream isn't worth worrying about anyway. They're probably just envious because it takes a lot of courage to follow your heart and your instincts, and it's not always pretty, and it's not always for the fainthearted, but it leads right into my next, and maybe most important tip, which is:

Don't be afraid to have a dream. Because one of the most amazing things about this life is that dreams can become reality, and I offer myself as living proof. With perseverance, faith, and luck—and by luck I mean, when opportunity meets preparation, truly incredible things can happen to you—I promise you one thing. It won't be easy, but it's easier than spending your life wishing that you'd done something, and feeling disappointed in yourself for never having tried. That's the true hell. So go on and do the thing that scares the hell out of you, because in this world, not unlike Hollywood, the gamble is almost as safe a bet as the sure thing.

And also, when you give yourself the gift of quietly believing in yourself, you'll love yourself. And now for another tip. It is of paramount importance for you to figure out as soon as possible that you must do things that make you love yourself. . . . Don't listen to things from yourself that you wouldn't accept from a friend. You wouldn't want a friend who wasn't supportive, so don't accept any less from yourself. You're only human, so learn to forgive yourself the little things, and do the best you can on the big things.

RUDYARD KIPLING

Born to an affluent British family residing in India, Kipling began his career in the 1880s as a Bombay journalist. He swiftly gained fame for his vivid short stories set in Indian locales, and by the time he returned to England in 1889, Kipling found himself already acclaimed as a brilliant writer. In the years that immediately followed, he produced such masterpieces as the colonial novel *Kim, Stalky and Company*, and *Just So Stories,* adventure tales written for children. In 1907, Kipling won the Nobel Prize in Literature. Two years later, he offered this fatherly guidance to his son John, away at school:

I won't bore you with advice. I know you will be good, but what I want you to do is be interested in your companions and your surroundings. Up to now you haven't had many companions, and you have regulated your surroundings to suit yourself. Now, my darling, you're in the world for a little bit on your own—and here's the whole secret of life—as you treat the world, so it will treat you.

Your esteemed parents do *not* treat you as you treat them, but the world, which is chiefly busy with its own concerns, behaves otherwise. If you smile at the world, it grins. If you frown at it, it scowls. This is knowledge that you will learn before a week is out. I merely mention it that you may recognize it when it comes along. Selah!

STEVE KROFT

Steve Kroft has spent more than twenty years with CBS as a news correspondent. He was named a co-editor of *60 Minutes* in 1989 and delivered his first report that fall. Kroft is the recipient of several Emmys, including a profile of then-Senator Bob Dole, and a profile on the tough, flamboyant mayor of Moscow. His exclusive 1992 interview with then-Governor Bill Clinton and his wife, Hillary, ended up on the front page of virtually every newspaper in the country.

After you get that first job, nobody is going to pay attention to your grades, or be looking at your transcripts, they are going to be looking at you. You may discover, as Al McGuire, the former basketball coach and broadcaster said, that much of the world is run by C students.

Woody Allen said that ninety percent of life is just showing up . . . and he's right. So imagine what you can do if you show up on time and know what you want to accomplish. I'm not promising that life is going to be easy. If it were, Zantac—a pill for heartburn, and Prozac—a pill for depression—wouldn't be two of the biggest-selling drugs in America. . . .

[But] if you love adventure and want to see the world, find a way and do it. It's becoming a smaller and smaller place, and by the time you reach my age, you will require a much more intimate knowledge of it. If you don't speak a foreign language, try to find the time to learn one; in an ever more complex and competitive workplace, it will become an advantage.

DAVID MAHONEY

David Mahoney was both a marketing genius and among the leading lay experts in neuroscience. Raised in New York City, he achieved swift success in advertising and corporate management, rising in 1970 to chief executive officer of Norton Simon,

Inc., whose holdings included Canada Dry, Hunt Foods, and Avis Rental Company. Starting in the 1980s, Mahoney philanthropically sponsored numerous neurological research programs. In 1992, he founded the Dana Alliance for Brain Research, a nonprofit organization of more than one hundred eighty-five preeminent neuroscientists, including Nobel laureates, committed to advancing public understanding of brain research. Mahoney's popular books included *Confessions of a Street-Wise Manager* and *The Longevity Strategy*.

Diversify your career from the very beginning. Stop thinking of jobs in series, one after the other; instead, think of careers in parallel. That means planning your vocation along with your avocation, and keep them as separate as possible. If you want to go into business, plan an avocation of music or art; if you are inclined toward the law or media, diversify into education or landscaping. If you want to be a poet, think about politics on the side, and study it seriously.

Don't confuse an avocation with recreation. Watching basketball on television, or surfing the Internet for the latest interactive game, can be a lively part of life, but it's not a creative avocation. And don't confuse a serious avocation with a hobby; do-it-yourselfing is fun, and so are clay modeling, and gardening, and fiddling with old cars. Hobbies are ways to relax and to make friends, and everybody should have some, but a real avocation is a subtext to a career, and a part of your working week to pursue with a certain dedication.

Why? Not only because it gives balance to your second quarter, but because it positions you for the time that will come, in the third or fourth quarter, to switch gears. And then switch them again—you'll have the time—and public policy will change to give you incentives to keep working or avocating.

George Martin

George Martin is best remembered as the producer of most of the Beatles recordings from 1962 through 1969. His actual credits are diverse, encompassing artists ranging from 1950s jazz bandleader Humphrey Lyttleton, the comic talents of Peter Sellers and Michael Bentine, legendary vocalists like Ella Fitzgerald, and rock acts as different as Celine Dion, Peter Gabriel, and Billy J. Kramer and the Dakotas. Born in 1926 in London, Martin has earned a knighthood for his career as a musical producer.

Obviously, talent is required. It goes without saying. Equally obvious is the need for constant application, plain hard work. Every first-class musician that I know works hard at his talent, not because he has to, but because he enjoys it. Someone like my friend Mark Knopfler seems to enjoy talent that requires no effort, but I promise you he practices on his guitar every day to keep his technique up to scratch.

Timing is everything. When I left college all those years ago, I earned my bread playing the oboe, but I wanted more than anything to succeed as a composer. It was the time of the grand film scores, and I thought if only I had a break, I, too, could write terrific film music. It was my idea of heaven.

Well, I did write for films eventually, and very different it proved to be to my imaginings. And a lot has happened on the way there. I had my share of success and failure, rejection, and acceptance.

I was lucky enough to join the record industry at a time of change, just before its big expansion. I took a job at Abbey Road Studios to give me a bit more money, and I became hooked on the fascination of recording. I was lucky enough to arrive at the right time, and to become part of a team that was learning as it was developing. It was hardly science in those days. We flew by the seat of our pants, and improvisation was the order of the day.

That timing, that luck, is something that we all need. Everyone has opportunities of one sort or another throughout their lives, and one cannot expect to benefit from every one. The trick is to recognize the break when it comes and to take advantage of it.

ABRAHAM MASLOW

Abraham Maslow is considered to be among the world's most important psychological thinkers of the past half century. His optimistic theories of personality and motivation, including the famous "hierarchy of inborn needs," have exerted huge impact on fields ranging from management and marketing to counseling and education. Since Maslow's death some thirty years ago, his stature as a farsighted thinker has steadily mounted globally. Lecturing about humanistic psychology to students at Brandeis University in May 1966, he emphasized:

The basic value question is: what vision do you aspire to? If you really look in the mirror, what kind of person do you want to be? Obviously, this doesn't happen by accident. You have to work for it, train for it. If you get a picture of yourself being a good physician, for instance, and of bringing babies into the world, such a profession can become a religious experience. Just simply an awe-experience.

Well, having that kind of thing means work, very hard work. Medical school is tough. Anything is tough if you want to be good. It's like asking yourself: What do you want to grow into? What does self-actualization mean to you?

PAUL REISER

Tenderly known to millions as loving, but very human husband Paul Buchman on the TV show *Mad About You,* New York–born Paul Reiser is also a writer, comedian, and producer. Majoring in piano before pursuing an acting career, he has enjoyed a longtime friendship with Jerry Seinfeld. Reiser is married to a psychotherapist; his recent humorous books include *Couplehood* and *Babyhood.*

In my experience, moments of clarity are few and far between, so when they do come, listen to them and hold on to them because they'll serve you well. . . .

I think it's true that you need to make a plan, set a goal and stick to it, but I would also advise: don't keep your eyes so fixed on your goal that you miss what sneaks up to surprise you, because magic will come from unexpected places. And I agree absolutely, don't let anybody get in your way. Don't listen to people who say "No" or people who think they know what you need. But, on the other hand, listen to some people who think they know what you need some of the time.

So now, with all these conflicting pieces of advice, how do you know which to listen to? Okay, this is where you come in. You get to decide. You make the choices, which is pretty much what I found out my first week in my freshman year at Binghamton. We get to pick our own courses.

It turns out you are actually in charge of *you*—pretty scary. Here's the good news: there's nobody who can do that job better than you . . . If there's anything else I can say, it's be courageous. Don't be afraid to bet on yourself.

ANN RICHARDS

Ann Richards served as Texas governor for four years between 1990 and 1994, capping a long career in political life. Previously as state treasurer, she was the first woman elected to statewide office in fifty years and initiated many banking and investment practices that brought significant benefits to taxpayers. Richards gained national attention in 1988, delivering the keynote address to the Democratic National Convention. Educational reform and environmental protection have been high among her priorities.

The first rule in life is: Cherish your friends and family as if your life depended on it. Because it does.

Number Two: Love people more than things. You know those T-shirts that say, "He who dies with the most toys wins." I'm going to promise you that over the years I've spent my life collecting a great number of things I thought I would die without. And I wouldn't give you a nickel for most of it today.

Number Three: Indulge the fool in you. Encourage the clown and the laughter that is inside of you. Go ahead and do it! Make some time for play, for the impractical, for the absurd, and make it a rule to do it. Not just every now and then. Let your heart overrule your head once in a while. Never turn down a new experience unless it's against the law or will get you in serious trouble.

Number Four: Don't spend a lot of time worrying about your failures. I've learned a whole lot more from my mistakes than from all my successes.

And Number Five: Have some sense about work. No one ever died muttering, "I wish I had spent more time at the office."

There is a wonderful world out there. It's just waiting for your energy and your ideas. We need you.

Securing a Democratic World

JIMMY CARTER

The thirty-ninth president of the United States is best regarded as a leader for his commitment to human rights and continuing activity as an international mediator. Indeed, for such achievement he was awarded the Nobel Peace Prize in 2002. Peanut farming, talk of politics, and devotion to the Baptist faith were mainstays of his rural Georgia upbringing during the depression. Though Carter's presidential successes were notable, in an era of rising energy costs, mounting inflation, and foreign policy tensions, it was impossible for his administration to meet high expectations. Since leaving office in 1981, Carter has authored several self-reflective and nostalgic books, including *The Virtues of Aging, Living Faith, Christmas in Plains,* and *An Hour Before Daylight: Memoirs of a Rural Boyhood.*

For too many years, we have been willing to adopt the flawed principles and tactics of our adversaries, sometimes abandoning our values for theirs. We fought fire with fire, never thinking that fire is better fought with water. This approach failed—with Vietnam the best example of its intellectual and moral poverty. But through failing, we have found our way back to our own principles and values, and we have regained our lost confidence.

By the measure of history, our nation's two hundred years are brief, and our rise to world eminence is briefer still. It dates from 1945, when Europe and the old international order both lay in ruins. Before then, America was largely on the periphery of world affairs. Since then, we have inescapably been at the center. . . .

It is a new world—but America should not fear it. It is a new world—and we should help to shape it. It is a new world that calls for a new American foreign policy, a policy based on constant decency in its values, and on optimism in its historical vision. . . . Our policy must reflect our belief that the world can hope for more than simple survival and our belief that dignity and freedom are man's fundamental spiritual requirements.

Nadine Gordimer

Nadine Gordimer is acclaimed as one of South Africa's greatest living writers. Her ten novels include *A Guest of Honor, The Conservationist, A Sport of Nature,* and *My Son's Story.* Gordimer received the Nobel Prize for Literature in 1991; her works deal with the moral and psychological tensions of her racially divided homeland. A founding member of the Congress of South African Writers, Gordimer never considered going into exile—not even at the height of the apartheid regime.

What do I mean by a fixed and unalterable sense of the right of human existence? Don't these change from country to country and ideology to ideology? And don't all countries and ideologies [claim] sole guardianship to them?

But I am talking of something comparable only to the middle ear in the human head, an aural organ but also the seat of balance, by which we find our upright. I don't know where the seat of a fixed and unalterable [affirmation] of the rights of human existence lies, and how many millennia of successive descents into and emergings from barbarism have gone to establish it—how many media—instinctive, mythical, religious, and philosophical—but I am convinced this sense does exist between fire and ice, the dreadful polar caps of human behavior.

It is not a mystery, it's a balance. We know what we are, we know what we might be. At the axis of these propositions is the sense of rights of human existence, and that sense is never quite lost. . . . [It] is there inside you, like your unseen middle ear: a collective conscience, a painfully arrived-at characteristic of your mankind.

JOHN F. KENNEDY

The youngest man ever to be elected U.S. president was John F. Kennedy in 1961. Leading the nation at the height of the Cold War and civil rights turmoil, his shocking murder left behind a glamorous legacy, "Camelot," unequaled in American history. In a time when many nations around the world were faced with a choice between Soviet intimidation and authoritarianism versus the U.S. way of life, Kennedy with his enthusiastic "vim and vigor" presented an idealistic, hopeful vision.

So let us persevere. Peace need not be impracticable, and war need not be inevitable. By defining our goal more clearly, by making it seem more manageable and less remote, we can help all peoples to see it, to draw hope from it, and to move irresistibly toward it. . . .

The United States, as the world knows, will never start a war. We do not want a war. We do not now expect a war. This generation of Americans has already had enough—more than enough—of war and hate and oppression. We shall be prepared if others wish it. We shall be alert to try to stop it. But we shall also do our part to build a world of peace where the weak are safe and the strong are just. We are not helpless before that task or hopeless of its success. Confident and unafraid, we labor on—not toward a strategy of annihilation, but toward a strategy of peace.

Seeing All Humanity as One

DESMOND TUTU

Winner of the 1984 Nobel Peace Prize, Bishop Desmond Tutu of South Africa worked as a high school teacher for several years before training for the priesthood. After two educational stints in England during the 1960s and '70s, Tutu returned to his homeland in 1975, appointed dean of St. Mary's Cathedral in Johannesburg, the first black to hold that post. After serving as bishop of Lesotho, he became in 1978 the first black general secretary of the South African Council of Churches. Tutu holds honorary doctorates from leading universities in the United States, Britain, and Germany.

How incredible that each one of us because we are created in the image of God are creatures of incredible worth, infinite worth. Each one of us is a stand-in for God. And so, to treat one such as if they were less than this is not just easy. It's a blasphemy. It is as if we were speaking in the face of God, and then we are created for God. We are this extraordinary paradox, really. The finite created for the infinite, but we are created for the transcendent. We are created for the beautiful, for the truth, for the good. And we know it.

Seeing Far Ahead

SIDNEY POITIER

Sidney Poitier is one of our country's most famous and enduring actors. His career defined and documented the modern history of African Americans in film. Growing up in the Bahamas, he moved to New York City as a teenager and soon began working for the American Negro Theater as a janitor in exchange for acting lessons. Some of Poitier's most notable films include *Cry, the Beloved Country, The Blackboard Jungle, The Defiant Ones,* and later, *In the Heat of the Night* and *Guess Who's Coming to Dinner.*

Only you can articulate the distance you are willing to travel to become the *you* you want to be at seventy-five. And me, the *me* I'd like to be at one hundred and three. If you agree that our journey's distance from where we are to where we want to be can best be measured by the size of our will and the passion of our intent, that's a good sign.

[But] life is tough. Damn right. Especially for those who tend to sit or stand on one of life's corners too long. However hard we look, we will never see as far as we should. However long we watch, we will seldom comprehend as clearly as we could. However much talk we hear of wonder, we will seldom experience her touch. The narrowest view life will ever offer of itself is reserved for those who never venture forth, who never travel those unknown roads.

Seeking a Fresh Vision

ALEXANDER SOLZHENITSYN

Among the greatest Russian-language writers of our time is Alexander Solzhenitsyn. Imprisoned in the Soviet Union for several years in the 1950s for his dissident views, Solzenhitsyn achieved fame for such novels as *One Day in the Life of Ivan Denisovich*, *The Cancer Ward*, and *The First Circle*. In 1970, he won the Nobel Prize in Literature. *The Gulag Archipelago*, his vivid exposé of the Soviet prison system, led to arrest and deportation. Following decades of exile in Europe and the United States, Solzhenitsyn returned to his homeland in 1995, and two years later, Russia established the Solzhenitsyn Prize for literature in his honor.

There are telltale symptoms by which history gives warning to a threatened or perishing society. Such are, for instance, a decline of the arts or a lack of great statesmen. Indeed, sometimes the warnings are quite explicit and concrete: the center of your democracy and of your culture is left without electric power for a few hours, and all of a sudden, crowds of American citizens start looting and creating havoc. The smooth surface film must be very thin, then, the social system quite unstable and unhealthy.

But the fight for our planet, physical and spiritual, a fight of cosmic proportions, is not a vague matter for the future. It has already started.

Seizing Opportunities

HANK AARON

"Hammerin' Hank" Aaron earned his nickname by clubbing seven hundred fifty-five round-trippers over his twenty-three-year career. Not only did he raise the bar for home runs, but he also established twelve other major-league career records, including most games, at-bats, total bases, and runs-batted-in. Aaron usually played the infield, but also gained recognition as an excellent outfielder, winning three Golden Glove awards. He earned National League Most Valuable Player honors in 1957 and appeared in a record twenty-four All Star Games. A quiet and effective leader, Aaron is now an executive with the Braves.

Watching all this coverage of famous attorneys, you students might feel a bit like I did the first time I watched big-league hitters up close. I remember having two reactions.

First, that given the chance, I could hit big-league pitching too. Second, that the difference between a .300 and a .280 hitter was pretty obvious. It boiled down to what the hitter did when he got *his* pitch, the one type of pitch he wanted to swing at. A .300 hitter would hit his pitch every time, but as often as not, when a .280 hitter would get his pitch, he'd foul it off.

The same difference seems to be true of most of what we attempt in life. Playing ball or practicing law, a person gets just an occasional opportunity to do something great. To come through in a big way. When the time comes, just two things matter. How well prepared we are to seize the moment. And having the courage to take our best swing.

PAUL REISER   (See page 177 for biographical information.)

I will tell you this. Life is short. And that is very true. You hear that a lot. It's a cliché, but I think it's very true. Think about it. Ten years ago, most of you were eleven years old. You were nagging your parents to get tickets for New Kids on the Block, and now you're graduating college about to set forth in the world. . . .

Life is short, so what does that mean? It means don't wait for things to happen. If you want something, go after it. Make it happen. As it says on my sneaker box, "Just do it." It means we only have so many years in this lifetime, so spend as little time as possible being miserable. It is your right, and in fact, it's your obligation to not be miserable.

Serving Your Country

DOUGLAS MACARTHUR

Douglas MacArthur is best remembered as commander in chief of U.S. military forces in the Pacific during World War II. Following the Japanese decimation of the American naval fleet at Pearl Harbor, MacArthur was recognized for his potent leadership as well as strategic brilliance. In the years immediately following World War II, MacArthur also distinguished himself in both Japan and the Philippines for spearheading effective and democratic reconstruction efforts.

Duty. Honor. Country. Those three hallowed words reverently dictate what you ought to be, what you can be, what you will be. They are your rallying points: to build courage when courage seems to fail, to regain faith when there seems to be little cause for faith, to create hope when hope becomes forlorn.

Unhappily, I possess neither that eloquence of diction, that poetry of imagination, nor that brilliance of metaphor to tell you all that they mean. The unbelievers will say they are but words, but a slogan, but a flamboyant phrase. Every pedant, every demagogue, every cynic, every hypocrite, every troublemaker, and, I am sorry to say, some others of an entirely different character, will try to downgrade them even to the extent of mockery and ridicule.

But these are some of the things they do. They build your basic character, they mold you for your future roles as custodians of the nation's defense, they make you strong enough to know when you are weak, and brave enough to face yourself when you are afraid. They teach you to be proud and unbending in honest failure, but humble and gentle in success, not to substitute words for actions, not to seek the path of comfort, but to face the stress and spur of difficulty and challenge. . . . They create in your heart the sense of wonder, the unfailing hope of what next, and the joy and inspiration of life.

Stand Up for Your Convictions

JANET RENO

Janet Reno is the first woman to have served as U.S. attorney general, and also held the post longer than any other official in recent decades. Born and raised in Miami, she is the daughter of investigative reporters. After gaining a Harvard law degree in 1963, Reno entered public judicial service in Florida and, starting in 1978, served as a five-time-elected state attorney general. Before her cabinet appointment by President Clinton, Reno was credited in Florida with juvenile justice reforms, improving child support collections, and establishing the Miami Drug Court.

Do and say what you believe to be right, don't pussyfoot, don't talk out of both sides of your mouth to be popular. Stand up for what you believe in, and be consistent. If people try to chop you down and you know you are right, stand there and be brave, and continue to state and act upon what you believe to be right.

You'll wake up the next morning feeling good about yourself, even if you sometimes lose, because I lost an election once. But I woke up the next morning and someone had put a biography of Abraham Lincoln on my bedside table—and it helps to know that Lincoln lost his first election.

When you lose, pick yourself up and move ahead, and you can still succeed.

Standing Up to Tyranny

WINSTON CHURCHILL

As British prime minister during England's "darkest hour," Churchill rallied his own people and countless others demoralized by Hitler's successes to triumph over Nazism. A brilliant leader and spellbinding orator during World War II, Churchill described his political role as a "walk with destiny," a destiny for which he believed he had spent all his life in preparation. His final stint as prime minister came at the age of seventy-seven, and Churchill continued as a parliamentary back-bencher into even older age. Besides leading his nation to victory over the Nazis, Churchill is remembered by historians as among the first to warn the West about the dangers of Soviet expansionism in Europe immediately following Germany's overwhelming defeat.

From Stettin in the Baltic to Trieste in the Adriatic, an Iron Curtain has descended across the Continent. Behind that line lie all the capitals of the ancient states of Central and Eastern Europe. Warsaw, Berlin, Prague, Vienna, Budapest, Belgrade, Bucharest, and Sofia, all these famous cities and the populations around them lie in what I must call the Soviet sphere, and all are subject in one form or another, not only to Soviet influence but to a very high, and in many cases, increasing measure of control from Moscow. . . .

From what I have seen of our Russian friends and Allies during the war, I am convinced that there is nothing they admire so much as strength, and there is nothing for which they have less respect than weakness, especially military weakness. For that reason, the old doctrine of a balance of power is unsound. We cannot afford, if we can help it, to work on narrow margins, offering temptations to a trial of strength. If the Western democracies stand together in strict adherence to the principles of the United Nations Charter, their influence for furthering those principles will be immense and no one is likely to molest them. If, however, they become divided or falter in their duty, and if these all-important years are allowed to slip away, then indeed catastrophe may overwhelm us all . . . [This] is the solution which I respectfully offer to you in this Address to which I have given the title "The Sinews of Peace."

Success Is Available to All

Timothy Russert

Timothy Russert is the moderator of *Meet the Press,* and political analyst for *NBC's Nightly News with Tom Brokaw*. He also anchors *The Tim Russert Show,* a weekly program on CNBC that examines the role of the media in American society. Raised in Buffalo, he holds a law degree, and served as a special counsel to the U.S. Senate before embarking on a broadcasting career. In 2001, *The Washingtonian* magazine named Russert the best and most influential journalist in Washington, D.C.

Reject the conventional wisdom that success is only for the rich or privileged or Ivy League–educated. Don't believe it. I didn't. Because people with real values have a way of helping and teaching and reaching one another. People with backgrounds like yours and mine can and will make a difference. In Poland, it was a young electrician named Lech Walesa, the son of a carpenter, who transformed a nation from communism to democracy. In South Africa, Nelson Mandela, a brave black man who worked his way through law school as a police officer, spent twenty-eight years in jail to make one central point: we are all created equal. . . . The future leaders of this country and this world will be born not to the blood of kings, but to the blood of immigrants and pioneers.

Sustaining a Creative Life

Paul Palnik

Paul Palnik is an artist based in Columbus, Ohio, whose posters and cartoons are infused with a warm spirituality drawing on biblical images and themes. The author of *Couples* and *The Palnik Poster Book,* he lectures widely on creativity and is currently artistic consultant to the Jewish Theological Seminary in New York City and its branch in Israel. Upon the graduation of his son Judah from high school in June 2001, he offered this advice:

My precious creative child:

As your father, I have helped raise you from the first day you entered this world. Creatively becoming who you are, deeper every day with a loving heart, is your unique plan. Only you can breathe your own air, give your own love, live your own life, and die your own death. As each day unfolds, strive to develop a focused awareness. Be strong enough to speak the truth and willing to fight for what is right. As you are committed to creative work, so also become committed to creative rest. Learn to start fresh.

Always give those who hire you "more good" than they bargained for. The path of creativity is a lonely one, until you learn to give your heart. Then it truly becomes a garden of delights. Giving one's heart is the basis of family, friendship, and community. Daily giving one's heart is the creative life itself, no matter what career you choose. Remember that dreams are not silly goals; they are your life's direction. Be certain that your dreams have a firm foundation in God. Learn from and respect the past, but do not turn the forms of yesterday into false gods. Experience each moment as fully as possible, and you will never be at a loss for what to attempt and express creatively in the world.

Taking On Responsibilities

MADELEINE ALBRIGHT

Nominated by President Clinton in 1996, Madeleine Albright was the first woman to be U.S. secretary of state. Prior to her appointment, she served as the U.S. permanent representative to the United Nations and as a member of the U.S. National Security Council. Emigrating as a child with her family from Poland on the eve of World War II, Albright earned her doctorate in public law and government from Columbia University and taught courses on Eastern European affairs at Georgetown University.

Over the years, many have come to think of World War II as the last good war, for if ever a cause was just, that was it. And if ever the future of humanity stood in the balance, it was then.

Two full generations of Americans have grown up since that war—first mine, now yours; two generations of boys and girls, who have seen the veterans at picnics and parades and fireworks saluting with medals and ribbons on their chests; seeing the pride in their bearing and thinking, perhaps, what a fine thing it must have been to be tested in a great cause and to have prevailed.

But today of all days, let us not forget that behind each medal and ribbon, there is a story of heroism, yes, but also profound sadness, for World War II was not a good war. From North Africa to Salerno, from Normandy to the Bulge to Berlin, an entire continent lost to Fascism had to be taken back, village by village, hill by hill. And further eastward, from Tarawa to Okinawa, the death struggle for Asia was an assault against dug-in positions, surmounted only by unbelievable courage at unbearable loss.

Today the greatest danger to America is not from some foreign enemy. It is the possibility that we will fail to hear the example of that generation, that we will allow the momentum toward democracy to stall; take for granted the institutions and principles upon which our own freedom is based; and forget what the history of this century reminds us— that problems abroad, if left unattended, will all too often come home to America. . . .

There is no certain road map to success, either for individuals or for generations. Ultimately, it is a matter of judgment, a question of choice. In making that choice, let us remember that there is not a page of American history of which we are proud that was authored by a chronic complainer or prophet of despair. We are doers. We have a responsibility, as others have had in [their times], not to be prisoners of history, but to shape history; a responsibility to fill the role of pathfinder and to build with others a global network of purpose and law.

WOODROW WILSON

Like Teddy Roosevelt before him, Woodrow Wilson saw himself as the personal representative of the American people. "No one but the President," he declared, "seems to be expected . . . to look out for the general interests of the country." A professor of political science and then president at Princeton University, Wilson later initiated many economic reforms including child labor prohibition in serving as twenty-eighth president of the United States. Due to his vigorous efforts "to make the world safe for democracy," Wilson succeeded in rallying a reluctant Congress and the American people to support England, France, and its Allies militarily during World War I.

Sometimes I feel that nothing is worthwhile that is not hard. You do not improve your muscle by doing the easy thing, you improve it by doing the hard thing, and you get your zest by doing a thing that is difficult, not a thing that is easy. I would a great deal rather, so far as my sense of enjoyment is concerned, have something strenuous to do than having something that can be done leisurely and without a stimulation of the faculties.

Therefore, I congratulate you that you are going to live your lives under the most stimulating compulsion that any man can feel—the sense, not of private duty merely, but of public duty also. And if you perform that duty, there is a reward awaiting you which is superior to any other reward in the world. That is the affectionate remembrance of your fellow men: their honor, their affection. No man can wish for more than that or find anything higher than that to strive for.

The Importance of Being Ethical

Tom Selleck

Actor and producer Tom Selleck was raised in the Detroit area, and won an Emmy for playing detective Thomas Magnum on the popular CBS detective series *Magnum, P.I.* His recent films have included *In & Out, The Love Letter,* and *Running Mates.* Once a campus representative for United Airlines, Selleck attended the University of Southern California.

Everyone thinks he or she is ethical. No, I'm not kidding—everyone thinks [so]. And why is that? Well, it's because we always judge ourselves by our own good intentions. We mean very well, so if we lie or mislead, it must be for a very good reason—otherwise we wouldn't have done it.

Also, we tend to remember the time we sacrificed something we really wanted in order to do the right thing, or took a big risk by telling the truth. But the problem is we all tend to squeeze these all-too-infrequent high moral moments for a lot more than they are worth. And while we may judge ourselves by our own good intentions, we are judged by our last worst act. If you don't remember anything else I say today—remember that. Few of us are as good as we think we are. And none of us is as good as we can be.

A father comes home from work and sees his son working diligently on a school project with this set of colored pencils that he doesn't recognize. He asks, "Son, where did you get those pencils?"

And the son replies, "Well, Dad, I took them from school."

And the father says, "Son, are you allowed to do that?"

The son answers, "Well, no, but Dad, I really needed them."

The father looks at his son and says, "I am very upset, I've always taught you to be honest. Why didn't you just ask me? I would have brought some home from the office." Then he adds, "You know I'm so upset with you, I think I am going to call in sick and go in and talk with your teacher."

The Importance of Faith

KELSEY GRAMMER

Best known for playing Dr. Frasier Crane on the hugely popular TV show *Cheers* and spin-off *Frasier,* Allen Kelsey Grammer was born in the U.S. Virgin Islands and studied drama at the Juilliard School of Music in New York City. For his *Frasier* role, Grammer won three Emmys and two Golden Globe Awards. His TV appearances have included *The Tracey Ullman Show, Girlfriends, Star Trek: The Next Generation,* and numerous *Simpsons* voice-overs.

It is my contention that to be successful, three things are required: talent, intention, and tenacity. Once a person has discerned where his or her talents lie, then a plan must be devised in order to achieve those talents, to realize those talents. The last part of the equation is the one that gets a little tough. Once we have decided what we wish to do with our lives and set out the business of accomplishing it, we discover that impediments exist.

Trials and complications jump out of life at the least opportune moments and tenacity comes very hard indeed without a sense of faith. . . . Work out your own salvation; do not become a sluggard in the race. Among you are the future movers and shakers of the world, the politicians and poets, the chefs and scoundrels, the artists and actors that will delight and confound us all.

Life will serve up staggering challenges as you go through it. You will find comfort and distress in the most unlikely places. In the eyes of a loved one, in the unexpected death of a good friend, you will find faith. The sheer beauty of the world around you and the laughter of a really good joke will sustain you. What you need most in life will be given to you. In the face of unimaginable anguish, there will be joy. I tell you this because I know it to be so. Take heart in that, and have faith.

The Importance of Humor

Bob Newhart

Capping a career spanning more a half century, comedian Bob Newhart won the 2002 Mark Twain Award from the Kennedy Center for the Performing Arts. His long-running CBS sitcom, *The Bob Newhart Show,* in which he played Bob Hartley, a successful Chicago psychologist, gave him unprecedented popularity. With an urbane, witty style, Newhart began his TV career at the age of nineteen at the media's infancy, when playing himself on *Toast of the Town.* His voluminous TV credits including *Murphy Brown, Rowan & Martin Laugh-In, The Andy Williams Show,* and *Alfred Hitchcock Presents.*

A recurrent theme running throughout commencement addresses is that what the speaker does for a living is worthwhile. So I will now attempt to justify what I do for a living. I was amazed when I re-read some of the books I had previously read on humor and laughter by the breadth of people who had written on the subject, starting with Aristotle, Plato, Hobbes, Freud (who devoted an entire treatise [to] it), Kant, Schopenhauer, Spencer, and Arthur Koestler, who devoted the first ninety pages of his book *The Act of Creation* to humor and its place in the creative process.

I've found that one other thing that humor does is make us free. That may seem like an odd conclusion, but as long as the tyrant cannot control the minds of free men, they remain free. Humor abounded behind the Iron Curtain and in POW camps.

Humor is also our way of dealing with the inexplicable. We had an earthquake a couple of years ago in Los Angeles, and it wasn't more than three or four days later that I heard the first earthquake joke. Someone said, "The traffic is stopped, but the freeways are moving."

Laughter gives us distance. It allows us to step back from an event over which we have no control, and deal with it, and then move on with our lives. It helps distinguish us from animals. No matter what hyenas sound like, they are not actually laughing. It also helps define our sanity. The schizophrenic has no sense of humor. His world is a constantly daunting, unfriendly place. The rational man is able to find humor in his. . . .

People with a sense of humor tend to be less egocentric and more realistic in their view of the world, and more humble in moments of success and less defeated in times of travail. I certainly don't delude myself that there aren't more important things to do in life than make people laugh, but I can't imagine anything that would bring me more joy.

The Importance of Teachers

BILL COSBY

An icon in the entertainment world today, Bill Cosby is one of America's most successful TV personalities. The Emmy-winning costar of the series *I Spy*, narrator of the cartoon *Fat Albert*, and star of the immensely popular *Cosby Show*, he has also been an active supporter of educational and civic causes. Cosby grew up in an impoverished Philadelphia family, and won a football scholarship to Temple University; unusual for a highly paid actor of his stature, Cosby returned to college in the 1970s to complete a doctorate in education, and ranks among the most popular commencement speakers.

You've got to lay it on the line. How many times have you looked out the window of the bus or car, and you've seen that teacher walking with these little people going to the zoo, going to the planetarium? What did you think about them? Did you see them in the classroom, or did you just think to yourself, "My God, what if she loses one?"

Teachers are God's children. And you've got to make that change. You've got to know racism and where it is in you. You've got to know bigotry. Where is it in you? You've got to know whether you have problems dealing with females, dealing with men, dealing with color, dealing with accents, dealing with poverty, dealing with middle income—[all] these people you have to teach—and you have to be pure and give them a fair chance.

. . . I think that had God created a teacher first, Adam and Eve would have been better off.

Understanding the Globe

Eric Freedman

Pulitzer Prize–winning investigative journalist Eric Freedman is a professor of journalism at Michigan State University. His issues are as wide-ranging as higher education and historic preservation, law and politics, spirituality and extinct species, corruption and creativity. Recipient of a Fulbright Award, Freedman recently served as a visiting professor of journalism at the Tashkent Language Institute in Uzbekistan. His books include *Pioneering Michigan* and *What to Study*.

Close your eyes for a moment and picture a map of the world. Good. I know exactly what you see. It's the map that hung on your own classroom wall, the map in your geography and world history books, the map in the newspapers and news magazines. You even know the color scheme—pink, purple, green, yellow, and brown. It's got the United States right smack in the center, Europe to the right and a chunk of China to the left. Greenland looks huge. It's easy to envision that Alaska, with its string of Aleutian Islands heading toward Siberia, is our largest state. It's called the Mercator projection, designed in 1569 by a German cartographer to help navigators.

But it's inaccurate—a terrible distortion of reality, a reflection of sixteenth-century thinking with widespread implications for how we think about our world today. Those distortions give an advantage to the European and Western powers, and give an edge to the traditional colonial powers over their former colonies that are now largely developing nations.

To make the distortions more tangible, picture this: In the real world, Alaska is smaller than Mexico, but not on the map we all use. In the real world, the landmass of the Southern Hemisphere is twice as large as the Northern Hemisphere, but the map crams the south into the bottom third. It misportrays Africa as smaller than the former Soviet Union, but Africa is actually one and one half times larger. Scandinavia is shown larger than India, but India is four times bigger.

Maps send messages. The implications of this map are immense when our mind-set and our knowledge base inaccurately reflect the dimensions of today's world. Ours is changing, where Asian and Pacific Rim nations such as Japan, China, South Korea, and India are gaining economic power, and where Western Europe no longer exerts the political, economic, and military clout it did not long ago.

As your generation begins to take influence and power on our globe, I hope you'll act with a new, more accurate map to guide you. The time is definitely overdue.

Using Technology Appropriately

TOM BROKAW

As anchor of the *NBC Nightly News,* Tom Brokaw is one of America's leading broadcast journalists. Born and raised in South Dakota, he has an extensive record of "firsts" with world leaders and events. He conducted the first exclusive one-on-one interview with Mikhail Gorbachev, which won the Alfred I. Dupont Award, and was the only anchor on the scene when the Berlin Wall fell. Brokaw was also the first American news anchor to report on human rights abuses in Tibet and to conduct an exclusive interview with the Dalai Lama. His books include the best-selling *The Greatest Generation, A Long Way Home,* and *Running Toward Danger.*

I envy you. You have at your disposal a dazzling assortment of new tools not even imagined not so long ago. The gee-whiz tools of communication and information: cable television, satellites, cell phones, pagers, faxes, and of course, the king of them all, the personal computer. Who could ask for anything more?

Well, here is a modest suggestion as you lead us into the new century. This will be the cyberspace equivalent of a teenage joyride, reckless and pointless, unless we apply the lessons of earlier technological revolutions to this one. They almost all have had unexpected consequences, and they are most successful when as much effort and thought is applied to the use of the technology as to the development of it in the first place.

If this new technology simply becomes another means of amusing ourselves, or of speeding the transactions of commerce or communication simply for the sake of communication, then we will have failed. If this new technology becomes primarily the province of the privileged, leaving the underclass to wander in cyber-wilderness, then we will have failed. If it becomes merely an instrument of greater invasion into our personal lives, then we will have failed. This is your technology. . . . This is your time. Take it on.

Using Time Wisely

ELEANOR ROOSEVELT

Eleanor Roosevelt, highlighted earlier in this book, accomplished a tremendous range of achievements. In her 1960 inspirational book, *You Learn by Living*, she offered the following guidance to young people:

Since everybody is an individual, nobody can be you. You are unique. No one can tell you how to use your time. It is yours. Your life is your own. You mold it. You make it. All anyone can do is point out ways and means which have been helpful to others. Perhaps they will serve as suggestions to stimulate your own thinking until you know what it is that will fulfill you, will help you to find out what you want to do with your life.

Each of us has, my husband's rather grim-faced ancestors pointed out, all the time there is. Those years, those weeks, hours, are the sands in the glass running swiftly away. To let them drift through our fingers is tragic waste. To use them to the hilt, making them count for something, is the beginning of wisdom.

Using Your Fears Effectively

CARLY FIORINA

Carly Fiorina is president and chief executive officer of Hewlett-Packard Company. Prior to taking this powerful position, she spent a total of twenty managerial years at both AT&T and Lucent. With a background in medieval history and philosophy from Stanford University, Fiorina serves on several corporate boards and also on PowerUp, a coalition among business, nonprofits, and government to give poor children access to technology and guidance on how to use it. For several years, Fiorina has topped *Fortune* magazine's list of the most powerful women in American business.

If you're scared today, let me ask you this: What will you do with your fear? Will you let it become a motivator or an inhibitor? Let your fear motivate you, not inhibit you. Ask yourself the tough questions:

Am I acting out a role, or am I living the truth?

Am I still making choices, or have I simply stopped choosing?

Am I in a place that engages my mind and captures my heart?

Am I stuck in the past, or am I defining my future?

And what will I leave the planet, in my two pages?

Tomorrow, you take your thousand pages and depart this incredible place. Before you leave, step back and consider the enormous text of your life thus far, and acknowledge its heft and its complexity. . . . I wish you luck, but more than that, I wish you courage and perseverance and the support of your loved ones.

Valuing Good News

FRED ROGERS

Fred McFeely Rogers—Mr. Rogers—was probably America's most respected children's TV host. *Mister Rogers' Neighborhood* ran for a phenomenal thirty years on PBS, garnering countless awards for its warmth and gentility. A pianist since the age of nine, Rogers majored in music composition at Rollins College in Florida. But after graduation, he became curious about the new medium of television, and did stints as floor manager for the NBC shows *Your Hit Parade* and *The Kate Smith Hour* before returning to his native Pennsylvania and marrying his college sweetheart, Sara Byrd. In the mid-1950s, Rogers created *The Children's Corner* at Pittsburgh's WQED, the nation's first public TV station, and became an ordained minister with a specialty in child psychology, while still holding his entertainment post. In 1969, *Mister Rogers' Neighborhood* began airing on PBS stations across the United States.

As I think about the kind of people my grandparents and my parents were, I remember one of my seminar professors saying that those who were able to appreciate others—who looked for what was good and healthy—were about as close as you get to God, to the Eternal Good. And those who were always looking for what was bad about themselves and others were really on the side of evil. "That's what evil wants," he would say. "Evil wants us to feel so terrible about who we are and who we know that we'll look with condemning eyes on anybody who happens to be with us at the moment."

That professor helped me to understand that mass communications filled with nothing but bad news can be very dangerous, ultimately deadly dangerous. I encourage you to look for the good wherever you are and embrace it. Yes, try your best to make goodness attractive. That's one of the toughest assignments you'll ever be given, but when all is said and done, I think you'll be glad you did.

Valuing Music

STING (GORDON MATTHEW SUMNER)

Among Britain's most respected pop performers today, Sting grew up in a working-class Newcastle family. He was a teacher, soccer coach, and ditch digger before turning to music. Forming *The Police* in his twenties, he led the band to global preeminence in the 1970s and '80s before launching his solo career. As the winner of sixteen Grammy Awards, Sting is probably best known for his song "Every Breath You Take" and a unique sound that draws on Celtic and folk, jazz, reggae, rock, rhythm-and-blues, and even classical styles.

Songwriting is the only form of meditation I know. And it is only in silence that gifts of melody and metaphor are offered. To people in the modern world, true silence is something we rarely experience. It is almost as if we conspire to avoid it. Three minutes of silence seems like a very long time. It forces us to pay attention to ideas and emotions we rarely make any time for. There are some who find this frightening.

Silence is disturbing. It is disturbing because it is the wavelength of the soul. If we leave no space in our music—and I am as guilty as anyone in this regard—then we rob the sound we make of defining context. It is often music born from anxiety to create more anxiety.

It's almost as if we're afraid to create more anxiety. It's almost as if we're afraid of leaving space. Great music is as often about the space between the notes as it is about the bar of demi-, semi-quavers that precedes it.

If I'm ever asked if I'm religious, I always reply: "Yes, I'm a devout musician." Music puts me in touch with something beyond intellect, something otherworldly, something sacred.

JAMES TAYLOR

Mentored by the Beatles for his first recording contract in 1968, James Taylor was first guided personally by Paul McCartney. Raised in an affluent Massachussetts family, Taylor gained early renown for songs including "Fire and Rain," "Sweet Baby James," "You've Got a Friend," and "Carolina on My Mind." Over more than thirty years, he has struggled both with tremendous success and problems involving substance abuse and mental illness; such difficulties destroyed his marriage to fellow pop star Carly Simon. Today, Taylor performs and records, still baring a tumultuous inner life through his music.

Music is a gift. It's a blessing and we really are the lucky ones to have music in our lives and at the center of things. Because as you know, music is the true soul food, and not that other stuff. You can criticize it, you can put a spin on it, you can analyze it and interpret it in terms of its cultural significance. But basically, that doesn't affect music. Music is beyond the fashion of consensual reality, and basically, it either connects with us, or it doesn't.

And because it follows the laws of the physical universe, it reminds us of the truth that lies beneath and beyond the illusion we live in. It gives us relief from the insanity of constantly trying to invent ourselves. And in this way, music is true spiritual practice. I thank God for music, and I thank music for God.

So render unto Caesar that which is Caesar's, but keep the money changers out of the temple, and keep music to yourself. I would advise you to keep your overhead down, avoid a major drug habit, play every day, and take it in front of other people—they need to hear it, and you need them to hear it. And persevere. The Japanese say, "Fall down seven times, and stand up eight times." So remember why you chose this risky enterprise.

Weaving a New Vision of Humanity

Vaclav Havel

Serving as president of the Czech Republic after the Cold War ended, Vaclav Havel is one of Europe's most respected intellectual figures and moral forces today. As a dissident writer, he was imprisoned for several years during the Communist control of Czechoslovakia. Havel's recent role as a public figure has now somewhat overshadowed his record as a dramatist and political essayist; his work often deals with the power of language to interfere with clear thought.

Many of the great problems we face today, as far as I understand them, have their origin in the fact that this global civilization, though in evidence everywhere, is no more than a thin veneer over the sum total of human awareness. This civilization is immensely fresh, young, new, and fragile, and the human spirit has accepted it with dizzying alacrity, without changing itself in any essential way. Humanity has gradually, and in very diverse ways, shaped our habits of mind, our relationship to the world, our models of behavior and the values we accept and recognize.

In essence, this new, single epidermis of world civilization merely covers or conceals the immense variety of cultures, of peoples, of religious worlds, of historical traditions and historically formed attitudes, all of which in a sense "lie beneath" it. At the same time, even as the veneer of world civilization expands, this "underside" of humanity, this hidden dimension of it, demands more and more clearly to be heard and to be granted a right to life. . . .

I have not lost hope because I am persuaded again and again that, lying dormant in the deepest roots of most, if not all, cultures there is an essential similarity: something that could be made—if the will to do existed—a genuinely unifying starting point for the new code of human coexistence that would be firmly anchored in the great diversity of human traditions.

What America Is All About

Dwight D. Eisenhower

Celebrated war hero for liberating Europe from Nazism, and subsequent thirty-fourth president of the United States, Eisenhower grew up in turn-of-the-twentieth-century Kansas. He spent his first fifty years in almost total obscurity, scarcely well-known, not even within U.S. Army ranks during the 1930s. But his rise to fame during World War II was meteoric: a lowly lieutenant colonel in 1941, he was a five-star general by 1945. As supreme commander of the Allied Expeditionary Force, he led the most powerful force ever assembled under one individual. During his presidency, Eisenhower ended the Korean War and sustained an effective policy of containment against Soviet expansionism.

Don't join the book burners. Don't think you're going to conceal faults by concealing evidence that they ever existed. Don't be afraid to go into your library and read every book, as long as the document does not offend our own ideas of decency. That should be the only censorship. How will we defeat communism unless we know what it is, what it teaches, and why does it have such an appeal for men, why so many people are swearing allegiance to it?

It's almost a religion, albeit one of the nether regions. And we have got to fight it with something better, not try to conceal the thinking of our own people. They are part of America. And even if they think ideas that are contrary to ours, their right to say them, their right to record them, and their right to have them at places where they're accessible to others is unquestionable, or it's not America.

What Really Matters

CHRISTOPHER REEVE

Raised in New York City and educated at Cornell, Christopher Reeve is undoubtedly best known for his movie role as Superman. *His other popular films include the cult-classic romantic fantasy* Somewhere in Time *and* Rear Window. *As a result of a horse-back-riding accident in 1998, Reeve suffered major neurological trauma and injury. But in addition to making remarkable personal improvement, he has become a major advocate for disabled Americans and their medical and economic rights. Reeve's well-received books include* Still Me *and, most recently,* Nothing Is Impossible.

There's a big difference between fun and satisfaction. And satisfaction will last you a lot longer than just having fun. There was once a show-jumping [riding] instructor, a man named George Morris, who was giving a class to a group of students who were jumping, and one woman was not doing very well. She was knocking down rails and not riding particularly well, but she had a big smile on her face.

George Morris said to her, "What do you seem to be so happy about? You are knocking down the rails, and you're generally riding quite poorly." And she said, "But I'm having fun." And he said to her, "If you would concentrate and really take this seriously and be in the moment, and really do this, you would have satisfaction—the satisfaction of knowing that you're doing your absolute best. And that would bring you satisfaction, which is a lot more rewarding than just having fun."

I bring this up simply because if you do something that is truly satisfying because it's what you really want to do with your life, it's your decision, nobody else does it for you. You go through the difficulties, you meet the challenge, you take on something difficult, that's going to build the platform of satisfaction, and it will be a basis for having a rewarding life if everything goes well. And it will also be a way to cope if things go wrong.

SOURCES

Aaron, Henry. Emory University School of Law, 1995. Reprinted in Andrew Albanese and
    Brandon Trissler, *Graduation Day*, New York: Morrow, 1998.

Albright, Madeleine. Harvard University, 1997.

Alda, Alan. Connecticut College, 1980.

Angelou, Maya. Lafayette College, 1999.

Atwood, Margaret. University of Toronto, 1983.

Baker, Russell. Connecticut College, 1995.

Barry, Dave. *Dave Barry Is Not Making This Up*. New York: Crown, 1994.

Bennett, Tony. George Washington University, 2001.

Bon Jovi, Jon (John Bongiovi). Monmouth University, 2001.

Bono (Paul Hewson). Harvard University, 2001.

Bowie, David. Berklee College of Music, 1999.

Bradbury, Ray. Caltech, 2000.

Brokaw, Tom. Connecticut College, 1986.

Buchwald, Art. Catholic University Columbus School of Law, 1977.

Bush, Barbara. Wellesley College, 1990.

Bush, George. University of Notre Dame, 1992.

Bush, George W. University of Notre Dame, 2001.

Cage, Nicholas. University of California at Fullerton, 2001.

Carter, Jimmy. University of Notre Dame, 1977.

Churchill, Winston. Westminster College, 1946.

Cosby, Bill. Teachers College–Columbia University, 1998.

Clark, Mary Higgins. Providence College, 1996.

Clinton, Hillary Rodham. University of Arkansas, 1996.

Clinton, Bill. Princeton University, 1996. Reprinted in *Graduation Day*.

Cohen, Ben. Southampton College, 1995. Reprinted in *Graduation Day*.

Connery, Sean. Cited in Andrew Yule, *Sean Connery: From 007 to Hollywood Icon,* New York: Donald Fine, 1992.

Corea, Chick. Berklee School of Music, 1997.

His Holiness the Dalai Lama (Tenzin Gyatso). Emory University, 1998.

Davies, Robinson. Dowling College, 1992.

Einstein, Albert. *The World as I See It.* Translated by Alan Harris. New York: Philosophical Library, 1937.

Eisenhower, Dwight. University of Notre Dame, 1960.

Ellison, Larry. Yale University, 2000.

Emerson, Ralph Waldo. Phi Beta Kappa Society of Harvard University, 1837. Reprinted in Wayland Maxfield Parrish and Marie Hochmuth, *American Speeches,* New York: Longmans, Green, 1954.

Ephron, Nora. Wellesley College, 1996.

Ertegun, Ahmmet. Berklee College of Music, 1991.

Fiorina, Carly. Stanford University, 1996.

Ford, Gerald. Tulane University, 1975.

Foster, Jodie. Yale University, 1993. Reprinted in *Graduation Day*.

Franken, Al. Harvard University, 2002.

Freedman, Eric. Milton (Mass.) High School, 1995.

Gass, William. Washington University, 1997.

Gates, Bill. Stanford University, 2002.

Goldberg, Whoopi. Wellesley College, 2002.

Goodwin, Doris Kearns. Dartmouth College, 1998.

Gordimer, Nadine. University of the Witwatersrand, South Africa, 1980.

Grammer, Kelsey. University of Massachussetts, 1991.

Giuliani, Rudolph. Syracuse University, 2002.

Halberstam, David. University of Southern California, 2002.

Havel, Vaclav. Harvard University, 1995.

Hawn, Goldie. American University, 2002.

Hemingway, Gregory. *Papa, A Personal Memoir.* Boston: Houghton Mifflin, 1976.

Hoffman, Alice. Adelphi University, 2002.

Hoffman, Edward. Alfred Adler School of Psychology, 1995.

Joel, Billy. Berklee College of Music, 1993.

Johnson, John. University of Southern California, 1996.

Johnson, Lyndon. Howard University, 1965.

Keillor, Garrison. Gettysburg College, 1987. Reprinted in *Graduation Day.*

Kelley, David. Boston University School of Law, 2001.

Kemp, Jack. University of Southern California, 1997.

Kennedy, John. American University, 1963.

Khouri, Callie. Sweet Briar College, 1994.

King, Billie Jean. University of Massachussetts, 2000.

King, Coretta Scott. Illinois College, 2000.

King, Jr., Martin Luther. Lincoln University, 1961. Reprinted in *Graduation Day.*

King, Stephen. Vassar College, 2001.

Kipling, Rudyard. In Reid Sherline (Editor). *Love Anyhow, Famous Fathers Write to Their Own Children.* New York: Timken, 1994.

Kissinger, Henry. Boston University, 1999.

Koch, Edward I. Quinnipiac University, 2002.

Koppel, Ted. Stanford University, 1998.

Kozol, Jonathan. Leslie University, 2002.

Kroft, Steve. Syracuse University, 1996.

Leguin, Ursula. Mills College, 1983.

Levinson, Barry. American University, 1999.

London, Jack. *The Letters of Jack London, Volume Three: 1913–1916.* Edited by Earle Labor, Robert C. Leitz III, and I. Milo Shepard. Stanford, CA: Stanford University Press, 1988.

McCain, John. Wake Forest University, 2002.

MacArthur, Douglas. West Point, 1962. Reprinted in Brian MacArthur (editor), *Twentieth Century Speeches,* New York: Viking, 1992.

Mahoney, David. Rutgers University, 1996. Reprinted in William Safire, *Lend Me Your Ears: Great Speeches in History.* New York: Norton, 1997.

Martin, George. Berklee College of Music, 1989.

Metheny, Pat. Berklee College of Music, 1996.

Mitchell, George. George Washington University Law School, 2002.

Moseley, Jonny. University of California at Berkeley, 2002.

Newhart, Bob. Catholic University of America, 1997.

Nixon, Richard. United States Naval Academy, 1974.

Omidyar, Pam. Tufts University, 2002.

Palnik, Paul. Unpublished letter, June 17, 2001.

Parks, Suzan-Lori. Mount Holyoke College, 2001.

Plimpton, George. Hampshire College, 2000.

Poitier, Sidney. Claremont McKenna College, 2002.

Powell, Colin. Howard University, 1994. Reprinted in *Lend Me Your Ears.*

Quindlen, Anna. Mount Holyoke College, 1999; Sarah Lawrence College, 2002.

Reagan, Ronald. University of Notre Dame, 1981.

Reeve, Christopher. Williams College, 1999.

Reiser, Paul. State University of New York at Binghamton, 2000.

Reno, Janet. Eleanor Roosevelt High School of Greenbelt, Maryland, 1996.

Reston, James. St. Albans School, 1948. Reprinted in *Sketches in the Sand,* New York: Knopf, 1967.

Richards, Ann. University of Texas, 1998.

Rogers, Fred. Chatham College, 2002.

Rooney, Andy. The College of Wooster, 2001.

Roosevelt, Eleanor. *You Learn by Living.* New York: Harper & Brothers, 1960.

Roosevelt, Theodore. Reprinted in *The Letters of Theodore Roosevelt,* selected and edited by Elting E. Morison. Cambridge, MA: Harvard University Press, 1951.

Rose, Charlie. C. W. Post, 1999.

Rushdie, Salman. Bard College, 1996.

Russert, Timothy. Providence College, 1999.

Seinfeld, Jerry. City University of New York, Queens College, 1994. Also, *New York Times,* September 15, 2002, section 2, p. 1.

Selleck, Tom. Seaver College, 2000.

Shalala, Donna. Syracuse University, 1995.

Shriver, Maria. Holy Cross College, 1998.

Smith, Greg. Berkmar High School, Atlanta, Georgia, 2002.

Spielberg, Steven. University of Southern California, 1994. Reprinted in *Graduation Day.*

Thornton, Kathryn. University of Virginia, 1996.

Solzhenitsyn, Alexander. Harvard University, 1978. Reprinted in *Twentienth Century Speeches.*

Sting (Gordon Matthew Sumner). Berklee College of Music, 1994.

Taylor, James. Berklee College of Music, 1995.

Teague, Bob. Reprinted in Reid Sherline (editor), *Love Anyhow: Famous Fathers Write to Their Children,* New York: Timken, 1994.

Thoreau, Henry David. Harvard University, 1837. Reprinted in Henry David Thoreau, *Thoreau: Philosopher of Freedom,* selected and with an introduction by James Mackaye, New York: Vanguard Press, 1930.

Truman, Harry. Reprinted in Margaret Truman, *Letters From Father,* New York: Arbor House, 1981.

Tutu, Desmond. Brandeis University, 2000.

Twain, Mark. Missouri University, 1902. Reprinted in *Mark Twain's Speeches,* New York: Harper & Brothers, 1910.

Underwood, Blair. Carnegie Mellon University, 2000.

Vonnegut, Kurt. Rice University, 1998.

Walters, Barbara. Sarah Lawrence, 2000.

West, Cornel. Wesleyan University, 1993.

Wiesel, Elie. DePaul University, 1997.

Winfrey, Oprah. Roosevelt University, 2000.

Will, George. Thiel College, 2002.

Wilson, Woodrow. United States Naval Academy, 1916. Reprinted in *Lend Me Your Ears*.

Winkler, Henry. Yale University, 1996.

Young, Andrew. Connecticut College, 1998.